HOME SWEET OFFICE

AF869807

HOME SWEET OFFICE

The Ultimate Out-of-Office Experience: Working Your Company Job from Home

Jeff Meade

Peterson's
Princeton, New Jersey

Copyright © 1993 by Jeff Meade

All rights reserved. No part of this book may be reproduced, stored in a retrieval system, or transmitted, in any form or by any means—electronic, mechanical, photocopying, recording, or otherwise—except for citations of data for scholarly and reference purposes with full acknowledgment of title, edition, and publisher and written notification to Peterson's Guides prior to such use.

Library of Congress Cataloging-in-Publication Data

Meade, Jeff, 1951-
Home sweet office : the ultimate out-of-office experience : working your company job from home / Jeff Meade.
p. cm.
Includes index.
ISBN 1-56079-240-X (paper) : $12.95
1. Home labor—United States. 2. Home-based businesses—United States. I. Title.
HD2336.U5M4 1993
658′.041—dc20 93-8563
CIP

Composition by Peterson's Guides

Printed in the United States of America

10 9 8 7 6 5 4 3 2 1

To Diane and Sarah Elizabeth,
with love

Contents

Acknowledgments

About four years ago, my wife and I found ourselves in the midst of a dilemma over where to live and where to work. I liked what I was doing for a living, but I didn't like *where* I was doing it. I remember sitting in my usual place of relaxation, on the living room floor, with my back up against the couch, when the thought first struck me that I might have an alternative to the office: home.

It turned out not to be so outlandish an idea, as I discovered in my research. Lots of people work at home. However, I might never have gotten my wish to take my act off the road in the first place had it not been for my boss, Ronald Wolk, editor and publisher of *Teacher* magazine. In spite of some initial concerns, he agreed to let me establish a long-distance relationship with the magazine. Ron has a reputation for being something of a visionary, as anyone who starts a magazine from scratch must be. I much appreciated his willingness to experiment with this strange and wonderful work arrangement. He gave me the opportunity to do some of my best work, and for this I am also thankful. By the way, Ron always said I couldn't clear my throat in 5,000 words or less, and I guess this is the proof.

I must also offer thanks to the editorial staff of *Teacher,* who quite unintentionally gave me the idea for the subtitle of this book.

Most of the time our editorial schedule was fairly hectic, so when a break came up we made the most of it. It was while working for *Teacher* that I first heard the term "out-of-office experience." We used it to describe our occasional road trips into the D.C. museum area or our lunchtime forays out to the Pie Gourmet in Vienna, Virginia. I don't know who coined the term—it could have been Maria, Jeff, Renie, Blake, Liz, Linda, Mary, or one of the two Davids, or, who knows, it might even have been *me*. I don't remember. But whoever said it, it bears repeating.

Credit is also due Frank Huband and Woodrow Leake, executive director and deputy executive director, respectively, of the American Society for Engineering Education (ASEE), who offered me the opportunity to work at home two days a week. Neither Frank nor Woodrow had ever worked with me before. The fact that they proposed such a relationship to a brand-new employee says a lot about them. I also owe a debt of gratitude to my editor and fellow cookie monger at ASEE, Patricia Samaras, for going out of her way to make sure the relationship prospered. I'll always be proud of my association with ASEE's magazine.

As I began work on the book, many people were a great help to me—far too many to list by name. Among the experts I interviewed on the subject of telecommuting, thanks are due in particular to Carol Nolan of Pacific Bell, Kathleen Christensen of the Graduate Center, City University of New York, Beverly Addante, director of Telecommuting Works, consultant Joanne Pratt, and Sherry Ahrentzen of the University of Wisconsin-Milwaukee for bringing me up to speed on the emerging phenomenon of home-based work.

I am indebted beyond measure, as always, to my longtime friend, colleague, and fellow author Denise Foley. Denise offered much-needed encouragement and advice to this first-time book author and many times kept me from crawling out onto a ledge. Thanks and love, too, to Eileen Nechas, former executive editor of

Rodale's *Children* and Denise's frequent co-author and partner in yocks. It was Eileen who dropped my name to Carol Hupping, executive editor at Peterson's, when Carol first mentioned that she was looking for an author to tackle this project.

I have always viewed with suspicion the standard author's acknowledgment of an editor's contribution to a book. After all, I reasoned—as most any writer does, in his heart of hearts—the writer does all the hard work. Heaping praise onto an editor always struck me as so much sucking up. However, I must say that Carol Hupping's influence is very much felt in this book. Although I've worked in newspapers and magazines for 20 years, I was a babe in the woods of book publishing, and Carol's advice and ideas helped a great deal.

Most of all, thanks are due the countless home-based workers and their managers who admitted me into their homes, corporations, and personal lives. I hope they inspire you as much as they did me.

Jeff Meade

INTRODUCTION

THE OFF-THE-ROAD WARRIOR

O, how full of briers is this working-day world!

—Shakespeare, *As You Like It*

The all-news station clicks on. You begin your day with sticky eyes, morning breath, and the news and weather. The news isn't good. The weather is worse. Have a nice day.

You head off to work. Though your personal haze has lifted, a thick fog has settled in. Soon you are jockeying for position on the interstate, hoping not to become sandwiched between a pair of semis as visibility drops to zero. Traffic moves like a New Orleans funeral procession, but without the music. Appropriately, the air is the color of a corpse.

An hour and a half after you left the house, you arrive at the office. The muscles in your neck are as tense as bridge cables. You down a couple of pain pills along with your coffee, and you settle in to tackle a long-overdue project. By noon you still haven't gotten past the first printout. Every time you begin to concentrate, the phone rings. Someone knocks at your door. The office manager pops in with a fax that demands an immediate response. Your boss calls what he promises will be a quick meeting. It isn't. It never is. The crash of the Hindenberg was better organized.

Does this sound like your working life, bunky? Maybe just a little bit? Perhaps every day isn't such a disaster. But for thousands, if not millions, of us, work is hell. Oh, the job itself may be just fine, perhaps even challenging, exciting, and rewarding—if you could ever get to it. But actually getting *to* the job, and trying to get anything done once you *are* there—aye, there's the rub.

But what if someone were to tell you that there is a cheap, highly effective, environmentally friendly, politically cool, and well-tested alternative, one that would enable you to bypass the superhighway, arrive at your desk rested and fresh, and be more creative and productive to boot? Would you consider it?

Of course, there *is* such an alternative. Two or three days out of every week, you could work at home. It's such a simple, practical idea. As Carol Nolan, home-based work czar for Pacific Bell, puts it: Move the work instead of the worker.

Maybe you don't think your boss will go for it. Possibly you believe you need a pile of fancy office appliances. Perhaps you always thought working at home was reserved for the high-powered executives, the fair-haired boys, and the corporate nuns.

Wrong, wrong, and wrong.

Yes, the right to work at home is often a perk accorded to the white-collar crowd. But increasingly, home-based work is an option offered to grunts, stiffs, and worker bees. All over the country, all sorts of employees—word processors, insurance underwriters, telephone sales reps, attorneys, transportation consultants, doctors, data-entry clerks, managers, book editors, telecommunications advisers, computer consultants, real estate agents, technical writers—are packing up their in-boxes and taking them home. The word often used to describe this activity is *telecommuting*—a confusing term in that it suggests something very high-tech and mysterious. But do you regard your *tele*phone as something out of the ordinary? In fact, most telecommuters *do* labor at computers, but for many, the most exotic piece of office equipment on their desk is the touchtone phone.

You *can* do it. And in this book I'm going to tell you how. I'll show you where to go for information, how to line up your arguments, how to overcome obstacles, and how to persuade management to give it a try. You'll find out how to set up your home work space and how to get organized. I'll also level with you about some of the drawbacks. Yes, there *are* some. But in my countless interviews for this book, I found precious few home-based workers with much to complain about. For most, home is where they are most productive. And by working a more flexible schedule, thousands have freed up more time for their families, enabling them to become more involved in their children's schooling, squeeze in the regular exercise routine that now eludes them, run errands while stores and offices are open, be on hand to accept deliveries or let in repairmen, and prepare dinners that don't come out of a box or a can.

No, I can't promise you that if you work at home you will experience nirvana on earth. I won't guarantee world peace, harmony and justice, an end to want, or even that the Mets will ever again win a play-off series. But if you follow the examples of the experienced telecommuters profiled in this book, you, your work, and your life could be vastly improved.

You can bring about this change. Let me show you how.

Chapter 1

The Ultimate Out-of-Office Experience

Like many young professionals who work in Washington, D.C., Susan Cook lived for many years in the northern Virginia suburbs, a sprawling colony of federal workers just across the Potomac from the capital. Each day she maneuvered her car into the slow-moving stream of traffic headed across the river, on the way to her job as a trial attorney in natural resources litigation at the Department of Justice. When conditions were favorable—no oil spills on the Beltway, no protests on the Roosevelt Bridge—the trip took 45 minutes; often it was an hour or longer. Like her fellow travelers, Cook was willing to tolerate this often trying commute.

Then she met the man who would become her husband. Her true love, a lighting designer for the Smithsonian's Air and Space Museum, had just closed on a house in Annapolis, out on the Chesapeake Bay, where he would never be far from the other light of his life—his sailboat. Says Susan, "He decided he'd rather drive a long distance to work than drive a long distance to the boat." So she followed him, his boat, and her heart to Annapolis.

Susan quickly discovered two things: one, her already grueling commute was now 15 minutes to a half hour longer; two, her new husband was an early riser, usually awakening at 4:30 and heading in to work before many people had tuned in to the weather with Willard. If Susan wanted to share the ride, as she often did, she would have to get up early, too.

Soon the strain of rising before the sun began to take its toll on Susan, who admits to needing eight to nine hours of sleep every night. Then the Justice Department began a pilot program permitting designated employees to work at home a couple of days a week. Without hesitation, Susan signed on.

"Frank had a fancy computer since he often did design work at home, so when this program began, it became obvious we could hook up electronically with the office," says Susan. "I decided to give it a shot." She began working out of her home on Tuesdays and Thursdays.

A Boomlet in Work at Home

Susan Cook, like an estimated seven million other Americans, is now firmly committed to working at home while remaining on the company payroll. Experts call this remote-control relationship "telecommuting," a fancy term coined by former aerospace engineer Jack Nilles back in the early 1970s (see *The Father of Telecommuting* at the end of this chapter).

Telecommuting is clearly *not* a new idea, though it has taken some time to catch on. Now, however, we appear to be entering a period of exponential growth. Spurred on by a range of concerns, from work-family initiatives to air-quality regulations, telecommuting is expected to get more of a boost as the decade wears on. By the mid-1990s, the number of telecommuters is expected to double.

Like many other people who work from home, Susan is connected to her office by a high-tech umbilicus. She communicates with her co-workers by modem (a device that links computers by telephone) and a fax machine, and she checks her office voice mail several times daily. "I can do anything here that I can do from my desk in the office," she says. "We have a big computer network, so I can access all my files. People can fax me cases to review. For my co-workers, it has become no different from walking down the hall and throwing the paperwork on my desk."

Susan began to realize that working from her home office along the bay offered other, unanticipated advantages. At the office, for example, she is plagued by constant interruptions. Home, on the other hand, is a retreat—a calm, isolated oasis far from the jangling phones and administrative brushfires. "On Mondays, Wednesdays, and Fridays, I'll go in and try not to have a set agenda, so I can respond to other people as they need me," she explains. "I get in at 8 and work until 6:30, and I really grind. But on Tuesdays and Thursdays I have a chance to catch my breath. If I have to write a brief or do some reading where I need to be undisturbed, that's when I usually plan to do it."

Like other home workers, Susan found this new arrangement gave her time to recharge her batteries. "When I first started working at home, I began going to an aerobics class," she says. "I lost ten pounds in the first six weeks. I was in great shape. I could also take the time to run errands—things I didn't have time to do on commuting days."

Portrait of the Home-Based Work Force

Here's a rundown of the whos, hows, and whats of telecommuters in the U.S.

How many Americans work at home?

Including those who are self-employed, about 41 million as of 1993, or roughly 33 percent of the adult U.S. work force. That's up from 27 million in 1989, according to Link Resources, a New York research and consulting firm that tracks work-at-home trends. Of these, 7.6 million are traditional employees who work at home some or all of the time, a net increase of a million telecommuters over the year before, reflecting 15 percent annual growth. That's about 5 percent of the nation's work force.

By 1995, as many as 11 million employees may perform all or some of their work at home in company-sanctioned telecommuting programs, according to Link projections. Telecommuting expert Jack Nilles further predicts that by the year 2020, 30 percent of the U.S. work force will work from home some or all of the time.

However, the actual numbers of home-based employees may be higher than statistics suggest. That's because many workers have informal arrangements with their employers that may not be noted in corporate records. Others don't fit official corporate definitions.

Until recently, for example, the Hartford, Connecticut–based insurance company Aetna recognized as a telecommuter any employee who worked at home three or more days a week. Aetna had 24 such employees that it knew of. But when the corporate human resources department surveyed company employees in the summer of 1992, it found many employees who worked at home less than three days a week. "As we interviewed employees, they told us about other people they knew who were working at home, with the consent of their managers," says Denise Cichon, senior consultant in human resources for the insurance giant. "There are probably hundreds of them. There's more we don't know about than we do know."

What kind of equipment do telecommuters use?

You'll find computers in 55 percent of all work-at-home households, according to Link Resources' 1991 data. About 27 percent of telecommuters have modems. Fourteen percent own fax machines.

Do women or men work at home more often?

Women, but men are close behind. According to research by Kathleen Christensen, director of the National Project on Home-Based Work at the City University of New York, 60 percent of all home-based workers are women. However, of all the flexible work arrangements now available—such as job-sharing or compressed work schedules—home-based work is one of the few alternatives to nine-to-five routines that appeals almost equally to men and women. By contrast, women make up about 95 percent of all employees who participate in job sharing.

Do telecommuters work at home every day?

Christensen, who is also professor of environmental psychology at CUNY's Graduate Center, believes one to three days a week at home is the more typical arrangement. According to 1991 figures compiled by Link Resources, of the 5.5 million telecommuters listed in that year, only about 876,000 worked more than 35 hours a week at home. The Bureau of Labor Statistics put the figure higher, however: 1.9 million people work at home every day as part of their regular employment, according to bureau findings.

The experience of Carol Nolan, head of the telecommuting program at Pacific Bell, is fairly typical. "Most of our telecommuters—and this has really surprised me—only work at home one day a week," she says. "I thought, when we started out, that people would get to the point where they'd start working at home three or four days a week. But it just hasn't happened that way."

Who is more likely to work at home: the executive or the executive secretary?

Link Resources found that 43 percent of all work-at-home employees are white-collar types—executives or professionals. About a quarter hold low-tech, clerical-level jobs. The rest are somewhere in between.

How many telecommuters have kids at home?

Just under half have children under age 18. In one of five homes there are children younger than six, according to Link Resources.

How prevalent is telecommuting among U.S. companies?

Not very, but the climate is growing more hospitable.

A 1989 survey of U.S. corporations, to which 486 responded, showed just 7 percent with formal home-based work programs. Nine percent said they were considering allowing home-based work, while an additional 14 percent said they had considered the notion but later rejected it. Fully 65 percent reported they had *never* considered letting employees work at home. The study was cosponsored by the Conference Board, an industry research organization, and New Ways to Work, a nonprofit resource development group based in San Francisco.

The numbers appear to be on the increase. Between 15 and 20 percent of the companies surveyed by the Conference Board in 1991 offered formal telecommuting programs to some of their workers. More provocative is that eight out of ten said they allowed work at home on an informal, case-by-case basis. In 1992, Link Resources found that 14 percent of large U.S. corporations offered formal work-at-home programs—roughly 29 firms nationwide.

Work at home was reported to be growing at the fastest rate in the following categories:

- Large companies with more than a thousand employees
- Much smaller companies, employing fewer than ten
- Executives and managers
- Scientists and engineers

If I Can, You Can

Until a few years ago, I never thought I would enjoy the benefits of the telecommuting trend. Then a series of events led, in a roundabout way, to my first opportunity to work at home.

Several years ago I lost my job as an editor in the Philadelphia area due to a layoff. After a mercifully brief search, I found a new job in Washington, D.C., writing and editing for a wonderful, exciting new magazine. My wife and I had always wanted to give Washington a whirl, so off we went.

We both found that working in Washington was every bit as thrilling as we had hoped, and we loved our jobs. *Living* there was the problem. As the days and months passed, we found that we longed for all our old friends, our old neighborhood, and all our comforting old routines in Philadelphia. In Washington, a city known for its rotating-door population of upwardly mobile professionals and policy wonks, we discovered that we just didn't fit in. We weren't cut out for the gypsy life.

For a while I started looking for employment back in Philadelphia, but I was conflicted. I really didn't want to leave my job.

Then one day it occurred to me that it really didn't matter *where* I was when I sat down to write or edit copy. I could do that anywhere. Why couldn't I do it in Philadelphia, from the comfort of my own home?

I started doing my homework, visiting the library, tracking down old news stories, and trying to piece together a proposal. It wasn't long before I had developed a small file on telecommuting. By the time I pitched the idea to my boss, I had all my arguments lined up like ammunition on a gun belt. I was ready for a firefight, and I was determined to win. But it turned out that I didn't need all the big guns. Very much to my boss's credit, in spite of some initial misgivings, he was willing to experiment. And that's how I became a long-distance editor.

Certainly, my line of work lends itself to telecommuting. But as I began my research for this book, I discovered all kinds of people working at home, for all kinds of reasons, including the desire for more control over their work, the need for a more equitable balance between work and personal and family life, or just fewer days risking life and limb on the freeway. I'll explore these issues in depth in the next chapter.

In a number of cases, employers are making it easy. A number of forward-looking companies now offer work-at-home arrangements as an option for their employees. But in countless instances, employees take the initiative. They do the research. They make the pitch. And because they do their homework, they're working at home today. You can do it, too.

Who's Who at Home?

If you really want to spend more time at home than on the road or in the office, you have to be prepared to march into the office and wow your boss with your deep understanding of this exciting new business trend. The first step in your mission is to gather information. You need to know more about telecommuting: who does it and how. Let's start with what you think you know.

To many of us, telecommuting conjures up images of pointy-headed systems dweebs or pampered, privileged executives, closeted away in highly mechanized cocoons, pounding out paperwork on the PC, communicating with the outside world by fax, modem, and voice mail. Their only regular human contact is the Federal Express courier.

This is not an accurate view, but it's what many people think of when they hear the word *telecommuting*. It may be precisely this skewed view that keeps many qualified people from pursuing work-at-home agreements with their employers.

Admittedly, the technically oriented *were* among the first to see the advantages of working at home, and they were in an ideal position to do something about it. "They're the people who like working with machines," says Donald P. Rogers, a professor of organizational communication at Rollins College in Florida who studies telecommuting. "They are usually the first to realize how they could benefit from those machines. This is also a group that tends to do the least hands-on supervising, so they usually don't need to be in the office. For them, playing with 'things' is more important than being with people. They're technophiles, and it doesn't really matter where they are when they do their work."

At Hayes Microcomputer in Atlanta, for example, product manager Lisa Volmar is one of a few company employees to telecommute on an informal basis. "There's a high level of PC literacy at Hayes, as you would expect," says Lisa. "I'm someone who can't think without a computer in front of me. It's very much a facilitator, and a lot of us have better computers at home than we do at work. Hayes has a very open office environment, which is a good thing in many ways, but it also leads to interruptions. I go home when I really need time to think without being disturbed."

Janet Reincke and her husband, Rob, both systems information specialists, were among the pioneer telecommuters at the Travelers, a large Hartford-based insurance company. Now a programmer in asset management and pension services, Janet began working at home back in 1985 after the birth of her daughter, Kristen. Rob, who works in the company's computer science division, started telecommuting a year after that. Now they work at home on alternating days.

For these two highly technical workers, remote employment came naturally. "At home we have two desks and two terminals," Janet says. "It's all set up in a spare bedroom. I can do better work here, where I have few distractions. It helps me when I'm trying to analyze things or figure out a problem."

After the computer types blazed the trail, less-technical office workers started to get into the act. Many companies began to see value in allowing their white-collar workers to do at least some of their work at home.

Chuck Hanson is a case in point. He's a market planner for communications giant GTE Northwest in Everett, Washington. In 1990, when Washington State established the Puget Sound Telecommuting Demonstration, Chuck volunteered to be one of his company's first guinea pigs.

His job was particularly well suited to at-home work, and after the demonstration ended Chuck continued to work from his home one day a week. "I'm an area administrator of forecasting. I try to project customer growth through the GTE service area," he says. "In my job I make a lot of telephone calls, and on-site visits from time to time. I live in Kirkland, in the area where I do my forecasting, so when I'm home it's easier to go out and see customers. Better to do that than to drive 30 to 35 miles into work, then turn around and go back out into my service area."

The Best Jobs for Work at Home

Clearly, not everyone who wants to work at home can do so. As Daniel Dreyer, a policy analyst for the Conference Board, says, "It'd be tough for the people who work on the assembly line at John Deere to telecommute."

On the other hand, many jobs—perhaps including some you might not associate with home-based work—are likely prospects. Here are some of the leading candidates for work at home, courtesy of Carol Nolan of Pacific Bell.

Job-Related Tasks That Can Be Done at Home

Accountant	Administrative work
Agent	Analysis
Analyst	Auditing reports
Bookkeeper	Conducting business by telephone
Broker	Contract preparation and monitoring
Clerk	Data analysis
Computer programmer	Data entry
Consultant	Data processing
Contract monitor	Data programming
Economist	Field visits
Engineer	Meeting with clients
Journalist	Research/planning/writing
Lawyer	Project-oriented work/client meetings
Manager	Reading
Realtor	Meeting with clients/research
Reference librarian	On-line database searching
Researcher	Support activities
Salesperson	Setting up appointments/research
Secretary	Typing
Tax preparer	Preparation of returns
Teacher	Lesson preparation/grading/reading
Telemarketer	Sales and solicitation
Word processor	Word processing

A Growing Option

In recent years telecommuting has begun to undergo a shift. Increasingly, many telecommuters are neither computer wizards nor white-collar workers. Working at home is gradually becoming an option for less-skilled, front-line support personnel and clerical employees.

In fact, one of the oldest telecommuting programs in the country was set up to help semiskilled working mothers. JC Penney, a leading mail-order house, established its own work-at-home program in 1981, starting with a core group of catalog order takers in the firm's Milwaukee telemarketing center. Since then the program has branched out to eight centers nationwide, with about 200 operators at any given time taking catalog orders from their homes.

All of Penney's telemarketing operators work part time, whether at home or in a center, explains Carl Kirkpatrick, the firm's planning and programs manager. Since the company takes orders 24 hours a day, some operators work days and others work nights. A center's telephone lines are set up to automatically divert a share of the incoming calls to those operators who are working at home. The company provides computers, which are hooked up to its mainframe, so orders can be logged instantly.

Having a small group of so-called "in-homers" gives the company more flexibility to respond to peak calling periods, says Kirkpatrick. But it also provides an opportunity for some young mothers to have a job while still meeting family needs.

"They're staffed two weeks out," says Kirkpatrick. "They know when they're scheduled to work, when to take lunch, and when to take breaks. There's no differentiation between those who work in a center and those who work at home. We try to take a consistent approach that they're all one and the same."

Cathy Kuehl is another clerical worker who has taken her job home. Cathy is a data entry operator for the Minnesota Pollution Prevention Control Agency. Her job is to enter hazardous-waste manifests into the agency's central computer. She used to do it like everyone else, from a desk in the office. But since 1990 Cathy has been happily pecking away at her computer from a new office, down in the recreation room of her suburban home, at a desk near the family pool table.

Cathy's agency inaugurated its pilot telecommuting program in November 1990, after one of the clerks in her office saw a report on home-based work on ABC's *20/20*. "She just wanted to start a program and see how it worked," says Cathy. Management agreed to a pilot program and chose Cathy as the first data entry operator to be permitted to work outside of the office. A highly organized and disciplined worker, she was more than willing to escape the everyday clatter of the office. "I wanted to do it for the peace and quiet," Cathy says. "Offices are noisy, and when you're a data operator, you have to concentrate on what you're doing. I thought it would be wonderful not to have the phones ringing all the time."

Cathy works at home four days a week, coming into the office on Thursdays for meetings. By her own account, the experiment is a resounding success. "I do about a third more work than I used to do," she explains. "I used to input about 160 to 170 manifests a day. I'm up to about 250 to 280 a day now. I just sit and do my work, and I get it done."

What's more, Cathy's employer couldn't be happier. "Her production is way up, and she's more content," explains manager Darlene Sigstad. "She's a very dedicated employee."

Clearly, many jobs can be done at home—not just those that require an M.B.A or an advanced degree in computer engineering. In fact, you may not even need a computer at all.

For every remote employee whose home office is so filled with machinery that it resembles the deck of the starship *Enter-*

prise, there is another worker who does his or her job the old-fashioned way, according to CUNY's Kathleen Christensen. "I'm convinced, based on the available research, that the majority use paper, pencil, and a telephone," she says.

Work-at-home employees often use their time out of the office as Susan Cook does, as an escape from workplace distractions. They go home when they need to think. And for this purpose in particular, the only computer many telecommuters need is the one they were born with: their brain. As Carol Nolan, telecommuting coordinator for Pacific Bell, told the *Orange County Register*: "Telecommuting can be as simple as taking an in-basket home."

Chuck Hanson has a computer and a modem, but he usually devotes his days at home to thinking and planning. "I might do some writing, but I mostly use the time for things that I can't do at the office because there would be too many interruptions. I organize my thoughts, and I try to outline what I'm going to get done during that week."

Particularly (but not solely) if your job is more idea-oriented than people-oriented, you could be a prime candidate for working at home. But before you prepare for your assault on the corporate status quo, you need to know more. How will working at home help you? How might it hurt you? Why do you want to work at home? All this requires some serious thought, as we will see in the next chapter.

The Father of Telecommuting

Back in the late 1960s and early 1970s, Jack Nilles was conducting research for a California-based aircraft company. The firm did a lot of contract work for the Department of Defense. One of

Nilles's jobs was to take a look at some of the emerging telecommunications technologies that were originally developed with military concerns in mind and come up with ideas for peaceful, civilian uses. At the time, he was also working with the National Science Foundation to come up with new energy conservation ideas.

Then one day he put it all together.

"On one occasion I just happened to be speaking with a city planner in Santa Barbara. He asked me why, with all our technology, we couldn't figure out a way to cut commuter traffic," Nilles recalls. "I guess you could say that was my 'eureka!' moment. I thought, Why not? Why do we have to be driving 15 to 20 miles to work every morning when we could be working at home?"

Nilles, trained as a physicist and electrical engineer, started bugging his employer to free up some research money to explore ways of using computers and telecommunications technologies as a substitute for those long commutes. "He asked me, 'What kind of people are you gonna need to do this?' I said probably an economist, a couple of sociologists, and a lawyer or two. He said, 'What are you, nuts? We're an engineering firm. We don't do that kinda stuff.'"

Shortly thereafter, Nilles left the company to take up a faculty position at the University of Southern California, heading an interdisciplinary research program. And soon after that, he landed a science foundation grant to explore his highfalutin proposal, which he called telecommuting.

"I had so many people asking me to explain what we were doing, and I'd give them the name of the project: Policy Decisions and the Transportation/Telecommunications Tradeoff. They'd say, 'Huh? What is that?' I had to think of a better word for it. So I cobbled together telecommunications and commuting, and threw in computers, and came up with 'telecommuting.'"

CHAPTER 2

WHAT'S IN IT FOR YOU?

Donelle Glatz was a benefits compensation executive for Crestar Bank in Richmond, Virginia, a long-time employee with a solid record of achievement. But early in the summer of 1989, as she awaited the birth of her second child, she knew she would soon face a critical choice.

"My baby was due in September," says Donelle. "I went to my boss in June, and I told him that I planned to come back in mid-November but that I just didn't want to work full time. I wanted more time with my family. We discussed the problem all through June. At first he came back with an offer for me to work as an independent contractor but at a lower hourly rate. I also wouldn't have job security. I said I couldn't do that. I would have to quit.

"At that point they put an ad in the paper for my job. We continued talking, but the assumption was that they would continue to look for someone to fill my position and I would quit when the new person came in."

Just when it began to look as if Donelle would have to leave her job of six years, her manager made a last-ditch effort to keep her in the fold. "He told me I could keep my full-time job status and salary and come into the office three days a week. On the other two days I would work at home. So now I go into the office Monday through

Wednesday. On Thursdays and Fridays I'm home. I monitor my phone, attend a lot of meetings by conference call, and look at a lot of spreadsheets by modem."

Thus began Donelle's unexpected new career as a telecommuter. Since then she has had few regrets. In some ways the job is now more demanding than it was before: Donelle generally puts in more time—up to 55 hours a week—than she did when she was in the office every day. Indeed, some studies show that the productivity of telecommuters goes up as much as 20 percent. A few corporations report productivity gains in the range of 35 percent. This boost in output is indeed gratifying to employers, but it isn't always a happy turn of events for employees. Longer hours can leave many home-based workers wistful for the comparatively easy life of the nine-to-five office grind (see Chapter 6, *Avoiding Professional Pitfalls*).

But even though she finds herself working more, not less, Donelle has gotten what she wanted out of the deal. She is able to spend more time with her children, taking her older daughter to preschool and ballet lessons "just like the other mommies do," she says. Donelle credits a caring boss for giving her the opportunity to achieve a better balance between her job and her home. "It takes a real family-focused manager to deal with this," she says, "because it *is* less convenient than having someone in the office five days a week."

Donelle Glatz is typical of many women in the workplace who struggle to juggle the often conflicting demands of office and family. Indeed, this nagging dilemma is likely to grow even more persistent. According to U.S. Census figures, more than 70 percent of all mothers in two-parent households have jobs outside the home. Women are in the workplace, and they're there to stay. And many of those women are going to find themselves faced with the same problem that confronted Donelle Glatz. A report by the Families and Work Institute, a nonprofit research and planning organization in New York City, predicts that between now and the year 2000, nearly 75 percent of all women entering the U.S. workplace will become mothers for the first time. In time, Donelle's solution may not seem so unusual. It is not, as we shall see, an ideal solution, but it neatly dovetails with a growing need among young families.

Indeed, family concerns are frequently cited as a reason for working at home. Not all those concerns revolve around children. As we of the "sandwich generation" progress through middle age, many of us are going to find ourselves caring not just for the kids but for our own aging parents. But people have other motives for telecommuting as well, including the desire to reduce the time they spend on the road, shuttling back and forth and sucking other people's exhaust fumes. Others hope to gain some measure of control over how and under what conditions they do their jobs. They find that they have their own unique style of working and being productive—and their way doesn't necessarily coincide with the traditional nine to five. Some people get more done in the peace and quiet of their own home than they ever will in their little cubby at the office.

What's in it for you? Let's explore the possibilities.

DOMESTIC TRANQUILITY

When CUNY telecommuting expert Kathleen Christensen began studying the emerging work-at-home phenomenon in 1983, she was intrigued by the potential for restoring stability among families.

"Back then, there was a very large push on. Companies were promoting work at home as a perfect solution for working mothers," she says. In fact, working at home often gives mothers—and fathers, for that matter—more flexibility. They usually have more control over their time, which means they can pay attention to family matters as the need arises—for example, meeting with the teacher on a weekday afternoon, staying home to care for a child's upset tummy, or chaperoning the kindergarten class on its field trip to the nearby potato chip factory.

"One telecommuter I know started working in his home office very early in the morning and took off in the late afternoon to coach his child's athletic team," says Christensen. "Depending on the degree of flexibility their employers have, working at home may give people more autonomy to respond to their children's schedule."

Finding Family Time

Michael Gitter enjoys this kind of flexibility. He writes and produces public information programming on cable TV for the city government of Fort Collins, Colorado, about 65 miles north of Denver. On any given day he may be creating training videos for city employees or marketing tapes designed to boost local tourism. He also administers the city's cable franchise agreement, resolving citizen complaints. He's been in the job about eight years.

Most of the time, Michael spends three or four days a week operating out of his home, in an office he set up in a spare bedroom in the basement. But it wasn't always this way. "When I started the job, I worked in the office at city hall, but there really wasn't enough room for me. The city was expanding, and we were hiring more people, and everybody was crowded into small cubicles," he says. "So to save space the city gave me the option of working at home. Since 50 to 75 percent of my work involves sitting in front of a computer, I said yes. I could easily do that at home, and I had always worked autonomously. I know what I have to do, and I do it. It doesn't matter to me whether it's four walls here at home or four walls down at city hall."

Though Michael didn't start out with the idea of gaining more family time, he was surprised and delighted when it worked out that way. He usually starts work at about 7:30 in the morning, throwing on some sweats and meandering down to the office. "I don't have to get up and shave and get dressed up. I don't have to go out and shovel the driveway in the wintertime," he says. "At first it was necessary for me to set some boundaries. I wanted my family to treat me as if I were at the office. I wasn't available for chores, to take out the trash or throw in the laundry. At the same time, it's unrealistic to expect that you can become a hermit in your own home. When it's time for lunch, I look forward to being able to come upstairs and see my son, who's eight months old. Whenever I take my breaks, my family is right here."

A Juggling Act

For Jeanne Eaker, a product support consultant with First Union Bank in Charlotte, North Carolina, the opportunity to work at home came in August 1991. She had been looking for a way to spend more time with her family, but her job didn't offer that flexibility. So about a year before she actually began working at home, Jeanne went to her manager and asked if there was some way that her job could be restructured. "I said this is not something I want to do today, but something I think the company should plan for. My primary concerns were to be able to give my children the opportunity to do the things that were important to them, and for me to be with them."

After some consideration and planning, and with Jeanne taking a lead role, First Union allowed her to begin working at home ten hours a week. She worked a regular schedule from 8:15 to 2:15 every day, but how she structured the rest of her time was up to her. The company supplied her with a laptop computer, which she carried back and forth from the office to her home, and she set up shop at her kitchen table.

"I have two children, and this schedule allowed me to pick up my daughter Sarah when she got out of school," Jeanne explains. "Sometimes I would take her to gymnastics or piano class. While Sarah was busy, I would sometimes take my other daughter, Katie, to the library, or maybe we would just run errands."

Jeanne worked with her manager to decide what aspects of her job could best be done at home, and the manager left it up to her to decide when to actually *do* her job. "I'm a very logical, structured person, so it was not difficult," she says. "I was able to do most of my work in the afternoons. Distractions then were minimal. I'd just start dinner and then go right to work. Sometimes I'd work at night. I made it a point never to get behind in my hours."

But even though Jeanne had more time to spend with her children, the job was by no means a piece of cake. With all the goings-on at home, she sometimes got sidetracked. And on those occasions when she was not able to complete her work in the afternoons, Jeanne says, she had to have the self-discipline to say no to a night of vegging out in front of the television. Her husband would put the kids to bed, get them their glasses of water, and respond to their little crises.

It wasn't always an ideal arrangement, Jeanne admits, but even though she has since returned to work full time—she accepted a new position—she believes she will eventually return home again. In spite of the drawbacks, including those late nights at the terminal when she would rather be spending time with her husband, Jeanne believes work-at-home arrangements are an important option. "In today's workplace," she says, "we've got to be able to provide a flexible environment for people who are juggling home and families."

Kathleen Christensen agrees, but based on personal experience and research she believes potential telecommuters ought not to enter into a work-at-home agreement unless they have both eyes wide open. Some start out believing their presence at home will eliminate the need for day care or in-home child care. But this is usually not the case. "I have a four-year-old and a 20-month-old," Christensen says, "and I work at home from time to time, but with great difficulty. You know, a three-year-old is not well versed in role theory. A child doesn't look at her daddy at home in his office and think, 'Now Daddy is being a data processor.' To the child, Daddy is always Daddy. Children need attention, so if you have young children in the house, working at home is *not* a substitute for child care."

Janet and Rob Reincke knew from the start that having their daughter, Kristen, at home during working hours made just about as much sense as lugging her along to the office. Nothing would get done. So ever since infancy, she has either been in day care or, now that she's older, in school. Kristen averages about five and a half hours a day under someone else's care. That sounds like a lot, Janet says, until you think about how long she might be in day care under normal conditions, with both Mom and Dad in the office eight or more hours a day.

THE LUXURY OF CHILD CARE

In a 1985 *Family Circle* survey of 14,000 women professionals and managers who worked at home, Kathleen Christensen found that roughly half had paid for someone else to watch their children while they were on the job. Presumably they could afford day care or in-home care. The same might not be said of those women who identified themselves as occupying blue- and pink-collar jobs. Of the women in Christensen's survey who said they were clerical- or secretarial-level workers, only a third paid for someone else to care for their children while they worked. The rest apparently relied on family or friends, or they took care of their children during the day and worked either at night, after the children had gone to bed, or early in the morning, before the kids woke up.

Not all in-home workers are allowed to use telecommuting as a substitute for child care. Many companies that offer work-at-home arrangements as an option make it abundantly clear that someone else must be watching the kids while the employees work. Pacific Bell's standard telecommuting agreement, for example, reads in part: "Telecommuters who work at home will manage dependent care and personal responsibilities in a way that allows them to successfully meet job responsibilities."

Bell Atlantic also advises strongly against using days at home for child or elder care. Bonnie High, manager of corporate telecommuting for the Big Baby Bell, puts it this way: "People will try taking care of the kids for a while, but they'll find out very quickly that they're annoyed by it long before the company is. We tell our telecommuters that right up front."

There's a magazine ad that shows a bright, pretty young mother in her tastefully appointed, high-rise home office with a gorgeous view of the skyline. She is surrounded by high-tech machinery, and she is depicted feeding paper into her home fax with one hand while she balances a baby on her lap.

What's wrong with this picture? First of all, most home offices are dumpier than that. My walls are decorated not with Laura Ashley wallpaper but with my daughter Sarah's art projects from kindergarten. I have a large papier-mache black widow spider hanging by a bit of string from my bookcase. There's a big flashlight on my desk so I can read the teeny little dip switches on my printer without going permanently cross-eyed. I have a friend whose filing system is anything but neat and orderly; she lumps piles of paper on the floor in rows alongside her desk. But where this image really falters is in its unrealistic message that one can easily juggle work and family.

The message you should take to heart is this: You *can* work with a small child in the house, but you *will* go out of your mind. Working at home does give you the flexibility to juggle your hours so you can spend more time with your loved ones. But you still have to work 40 or 50 hours a week. Your work has to be done sometime, and it won't happen while you are playing Pony Boy.

The sooner you realize this, the better off you'll be. For many people, that extra flexibility is worth some of the sacrifices they will have to make. As Kathleen Christensen says, "While work at home is not the perfect solution to balancing work and family, it may solve some problems."

A Measure of Independence

When it comes to good old-fashioned brainwork, there's no place like home. On those occasions when you need peace and quiet, the office may provide too many distractions.

"Managers often buy the myth that the best place to do office work is in the office," says Gil Gordon, a New Jersey–based telecommuting consultant and editor of the national newsletter

Telecommuting Review. "In many cases the office is the worst place. There's noise, and there are constant distractions."

To many managers this may seem like heresy. But now, with the rise of telecommuting, more and more employees are opting to do their work where and when they believe they work best. "People want to work at home for reasons related to their lifestyle," Kathleen Christensen concedes, "but their reasons may also be related to their own particular style of working. They may want to work at their own pace. It's an issue of control and autonomy."

Marylee Newman is a registered nurse who works as a medical underwriter for Blue Cross and Blue Shield in Washington, D.C. She works from her suburban Pooleville, Maryland, home three days a week, visiting the office on Tuesdays and Thursdays. When her company offered her the opportunity to work at home as part of a pilot work-family initiative, she signed on. One reason was her desire to spend more time with her young sons, Teddy and Philip. But another personal priority was the desire to work on her own terms.

"I end up doing more work than I did when I was in the office every day," Marylee says. "I roll out of bed and get right to work. I can control my time. I sit down at my desk and hammer out a tremendous amount of work. After that, I'll take a two-hour break. Then, when I come back, I quickly refocus and continue working."

It isn't as easy as it might seem, as Marylee is the first to admit. "The individual who does this has to be strongly organized and disciplined. You have to stay totally in control."

Attorney Susan Cook believed she was exactly that kind of worker—self-motivated, highly disciplined, well organized. But it was not until she began working at home that she discovered how useful these skills really were.

"I have a tendency to be real organized. My husband calls it 'compulsive.' But when I started working at home, I became even better organized than I was before. Working at home got me into better time-planning habits. I keep detailed calendars and long lists of things to do. I plan out what I'm going to do every day of the week. I operate a lot better. I'm more productive. My stress level goes down, and my job satisfaction goes way up."

Tina Koyama was newsletter editor for Seattle Metro, a public transit and water pollution control agency, when the state of Washington inaugurated the Puget Sound Telecommuting Demonstration to test the feasibility of work at home. Koyama grabbed the chance to work at home one day a week precisely because the office sometimes interfered with her ability to get her work done. "At work a lot of my job requires being available to other employees, but it's also really interruptive. At home I found I could concentrate more easily. There were no drop-in interruptions. At work I sat in a cubicle, and people would just drop by and start talking to me. Well, being with people is an important part of work, but when you're working on a story, it's hard to concentrate."

To some people, of course, it's hard to believe you can get anything done at home, a place virtually overflowing with distractions. Tina's co-workers used to joke that she was really watching *I Love Lucy* when they called. But Tina managed to steer clear of the TV set. She set her own pace, which at times bordered on blistering. "I'm a real morning person," she explains. "Because I was at home, I could start my workday at 6 A.M., during the time I worked best, and I had the option of knocking off early. Because I was so well motivated, I really got things done much faster. Often I'd get done a lot sooner than I expected."

Suzanne Smith, co-director of New Ways to Work, a San Francisco–based nonprofit resource development group, believes strongly in giving individuals more control over the circumstances of their job, but she believes such negotiations call for a certain level of sophistication on the part of workers *and* management: "The one thing we have really learned, over years of experience, is that there are reasons for being together as a group and reasons for being apart. If we can become more sophisticated in our work, we can design it so that we may be apart for the kind of work that can best be done that way."

Are You Cut Out for Work at Home?

All the benefits you've been reading about may make telecommuting sound very attractive to you. But before you get hooked on the idea, take a few minutes to see if it's right not just for you but for your job.

Count yourself out if you manage a large staff that requires your constant supervision. If not, answer the following:

How much person-to-person contact does your job involve?
- 1= A lot
- 2= Some
- 3= Little or none

How much of your work is done over the phone?
- 1= Very little
- 2= A moderate amount
- 3= Most or all of it

Do you set goals and clear objectives?
- 1= Rarely
- 2= Sometimes
- 3= Always

If you set goals, do you meet them?
- 1= Rarely
- 2= Most of the time
- 3= Always

In your most recent evaluation, did you exceed expectations for productivity?
- 1= No—I didn't meet expectations.
- 2= No—I met them, but just barely.
- 3= Yes, I exceeded expectations.

Does your job require close, constant supervision, or do you control the pace of your work?
- 1= Close supervision
- 2= Some supervision, some independence
- 3= I set the pace

Do you work well in isolation?
- 1= No. I'm a people person.
- 2= Sometimes, but I also need to be around others.

3= Yes. I don't need constant interaction.

If you are allowed to work at home, describe what child or dependent care arrangements you'll make.

1= I will assume full responsibility for child or dependent care.
2= Small children or older adults will be under someone else's care some of the time.
3= Small children or older adults will be under someone else's care whenever I need to work. (Give yourself three points if you have no children or adults to take care of.)

How long have you been in your present job or with your present company?

1= 0 to 2 years
2= 3 to 5 years
3= 6 or more years

Describe your home office.

1= What office? We're crammed.
2= It's in my bedroom, kitchen, or living room, in the midst of the family's usual traffic pattern.
3= It's in a spare bedroom, den, or room in the basement or garage, away from my main living area.

Scoring: 10–19 Don't give up your office job.
20–25 You're a potential candidate, but you may need to make some changes to appeal to your boss.
26–30 You're ideally suited. What are you waiting for?

Freedom From the Road—and Cleaner Air

Many of us spend more time on the road, going to and from work, than we imagine. But to get an idea of how many hours are wasted commuting, consider this example from the Los Angeles area, where one-hour, one-way drives are all too typical. According to Commuter Transportation Services, Inc., if a fraction of L.A.'s carbound commuters—just 5 percent— worked at home one day a week, they would wind up driving 205 million miles less every year.

Car Talk

Paul and Sarah Edwards, two of the leading experts on home-based work, point out in *Working From Home: Everything You Need to Know About Living and Working Under the Same Roof* (Jeremy P. Tarcher, Inc.) that if you commute just 20 minutes one way, five days a week, by the end of the year you will have devoted 160 hours to commuting. Happy motoring!

Reducing workers' time on the road was one of the motives behind Bell Atlantic's telecommuting program. "Some people are really into hellacious commutes," says Bonnie High. "It's no treat to be on the road an hour and a half. That utilizes energy that could be better used in other ways. On the days when I work at home I have a two- to three-second commute. So I ask you, who's got the most energy, and who is going to be most productive?"

By working at home one day a week, GTE market planner Chuck Hanson cut the number of hours he spends on the road each week. "For me, it's about a 30- to 35-mile drive into the office, and it's getting more and more congested," he says. Now, on the day he stays home, Hanson is able to start work right away, at a time when everyone else is out pushing their way through heavy traffic at the nearby Boeing plant.

Of course, not all of us commute by car. Tina Koyama, who was Chuck Hanson's crosstown colleague in the Puget Sound telecommuting experiment, takes the bus, a 12-mile, stop-and-go trip that takes 45 minutes on a good day. She found that eliminating that commute, if only for one day a week, vastly improved her outlook on life. "Sitting there in traffic, day after day, is just stressful," she says. "I found that on the day I chose to stay home, I felt a lot less tired."

The Clean Air Act Likes Telecommuters

The ability to declare your independence from the bondage of the automobile is one of the great advantages of working at home. But commuting is more than just a drag and a waste of time. It's also one terrific way to burn humongous, continent-size holes in the ozone layer, the atmospheric shield that protects us all from being turned into charbroiled steak as a result of ultraviolet radiation. Soon, like it or not, corporate America is going to get on the work-at-home bandwagon, not just because the Suits have come to realize that freeway driving wastes your time, but because the government frowns on wanton atmospheric destruction.

Companies in the nation's grimiest, most polluted cities are now expected to comply with the requirements of the federal Clean Air Act, passed by Congress in 1992. The cities voted Most Likely to Have to Clean Up Their Act include Los Angeles, San Diego, Philadelphia, Chicago, Houston, Milwaukee, Baltimore-Washington, and the New York City–Northern New Jersey corridor. The feds are requiring companies with 100 or more employees to reduce commuting by auto by a whopping 25 percent. The companies' plans have to be in effect no later than 1996.

Of course, companies don't have limitless options. According to telecommuting expert Jack Nilles, "When a company is faced with a regulation that says they have to get people out of their cars, the first thing they tend to do is increase the number of car pools. That's relatively simple. They can also charge people for parking if they're not part of a car pool. But regardless of what they do, those measures alone don't do enough to knock down the number of single-driver cars. So what companies usually do next is initiate van pools. But this is less than a perfect solution. It usually requires a substantial cash investment on the company's part. And as a practical matter, historically even fewer people join van pools than join car pools.

Typically, the number of people in van pools is 10 to 20 percent of the people who join car pools."

Working at home is the one option companies could offer that would cost them relatively little money and would likely be supported by most employees, Nilles says. But it takes most companies some time to get to that point. "Only when all other approaches fail to work do executives reach the desperate point where they say, 'Maybe we don't need to have everybody come to work every day.'"

If past experience is any indication, an increase in telecommuting is likely to eventually follow imposition of federal clean-air regulations. According to a report in the *Wall Street Journal,* auto travel to and from work dropped 12 percent in Phoenix, mostly as a result of increased telecommuting, following enactment of strict local air-pollution laws in 1988.

Getting motorists off the road—but for reasons unrelated to the environment—was one of the driving forces, so to speak, behind an L.A. initiative in 1984. That's the year the Olympics came to La-La Land. The local Olympic organizing committee asked center-city businesses to reduce employee traffic to make room for the expected increase in visitor autos. "They sent out an edict to all the businesses in downtown L.A.," says Carol Nolan, head of telecommuting at Pacific Bell. "With the size of our business, there wasn't a whole lot we could do. We have offices all over creation. There's a friendly phone company office in every neighborhood."

So Pac Bell initiated its first formal telecommuting program, getting employees out of their downtown offices and into offices in the surrounding suburbs or, whenever possible, in their own homes. "The response from our employees was very favorable," says Nolan. "So after the Olympics, the corporation considered whether this was something we needed to continue. We put together a task force for a pilot project in 1985, with about 100 employees. In 1989 we formalized the policy, and the program has just continued to grow." Pac Bell now employs an estimated 1,500 telecommuters.

Less Time in Your Car, More Time at Home

As the smog cloud continues to grow, obscuring more and more of southern California's once azure skies, the effort to get more workers off the road and into their own homes is expected to gain even further impetus. One thing is for sure: Whether for reasons of personal convenience or environmental health and safety, your car is likely to spend more time in the garage—and you will probably spend more time at home—in the very near future.

None of which would be the least bit surprising to Bell Atlantic's Bonnie High.

"I have felt strongly about working at home since I was a child, believe it or not," says High, herself a confirmed remote worker. "When I was a kid, I used to watch *The Jetsons.* Even then I understood the concept of people someday working at home, and I used to tell my mother, 'This is the way it should be.' Now I'm living to see all this come to fruition."

The Good and the Bad

It may be comforting to think of home-based work as the solution to all your problems. Having the luxury of time at home *does* solve some problems, no question. But as with many choices you make, it has consequences, not all of them good.

Sherry Ahrentzen, associate professor of architecture at the University of Wisconsin-Milwaukee, conducted a survey of home-based workers to determine what they liked—and didn't like—about working at home. Here are some of her findings.

The Good Points:

Flexibility. Your time is your own, much more so than in the conventional office setting. You can arise at 5 A.M., start to work immediately, and wrap up before the kids get home from school. Or you can work a normal schedule until 3 P.M., pick up the kids, feed them their snacks, maybe walk down to the park for an afternoon of teeter-tottering, and make up the time later, when the kids are in bed.

Freedom. People who work at home have greater independence than their office-bound colleagues. When you work a straight nine-to-five schedule, you have less control over your life. You have to live by someone else's terms, which means taking time to go to the dentist or have a parent-teacher conference only when it meets the needs of your employer. People who work at home decide what to do when.

Coziness. Dorothy said it best: There's no place like home. When you work at home, you have all the comforting trappings of home life—your couch, your La-Z-Boy, your kitchen table, your tree-lined neighborhood streets—and none of the drawbacks of the often sterile office environment, where you might not even be allowed to decorate the walls.

Strictly informal attire. No suits, no high heels. When you work at home, you can dress in a comfortable flannel shirt, jeans, and Top-siders. No one know or cares how you look.

You work smarter. Most telecommuters say they become more productive when they work at home. That's because they leave many of the most common, frustrating interruptions at the office.

No commute. Pitch the Pinto. Park the Ranger in the garage. When you bring your work home with you, there's no need to head out onto the highway.

The Bad Points:

Chaos at home. You bring your work home with you, looking forward to settling in to study that new proposal in depth. At least you *would* study it if your son had not chosen to color all over it. Working at home often is sometimes at odds with normal home life.

Loneliness. You really wanted to get away from the office. Thought you could get more work done. Well, that's true. You're more productive than ever. But once you leave the office setting, you find you often miss the familiar give-and-take of the workplace. You lose track of who's doing what to whom.

Exhaustion. People who work at home are often so grateful to be there, free of the usual encumbrances, that they work harder than they ever have. At first it's thrilling, exciting. The boss heaps praise on you. But soon it becomes very hard indeed. More work is good for your employer—but bad, sometimes, for you.

Professional Jeopardy. I'll take loss of opportunities for advancement for $500, Alex. Work at home and you could work your way out of your boss's alleged memory. If you only work at home a day or two a week, generally there's no problem. But if you set up shop in your spare bedroom more than that, you could throw a monkey wrench into your career. Your boss finds herself thinking things like this: "Now where was that up-and-coming insurance underwriter, anyway? I know she *used* to work here...." (For more on this subject, see Chapter 6.)

Why You'll Like Home-Based Work

- Work on your own terms—when working at home, you can choose where and when you want to work (within reason!).
- Fewer interruptions—no meetings, fewer phone calls, and no office banter will mean you can get more work done; this is especially good news when a project needs your full attention.
- Less commuting—less wear and tear on your car (and you); less money spent for gas or public transportation; less time on the road.
- More time for yourself and your family—you can be there after school, exercise at lunch (and take a shower afterward!), let in the plumber, make a real dinner....
- No dressing up on days at home—less money and effort spent on office clothes.
- No buying lunch or packing one to take to work—save money and eat up the leftovers.
- A change of pace and environment that can break up the routine of the workweek.

CHAPTER 3

WHAT'S IN IT FOR YOUR BOSS?

Why should you care whether the company benefits from your desire to work at home? What's important is whether you get what *you* want. Right?

Right—but only to a point. If your telecommuting proposal seems decidedly lopsided in your favor, then you may *never* get to work at home. To be successful you'll have to persuade your employer that there's something to be gained on both sides. If you can get your supervisor excited about the potential work-related benefits of a telecommuting arrangement, then you stand a better chance of achieving your personal goals. Bear in mind that what benefits your employer ultimately benefits you. Many of the points discussed in this chapter can be turned into ammunition to bolster your case.

Before Bell Atlantic began its first six-month pilot program in telecommuting in February 1991, many other companies already had work-at-home policies in place. But while other firms had dived right in, Bell Atlantic was determined to avoid some of the problems that had nearly deep-sixed those other corporate efforts, including hard-headed resistance among managers and misunderstanding and resentment among workers. So Bell Atlantic not only ran one six-month pilot but dabbled its piggies in the water for another six months just to make sure most of the problems had been worked out.

Maybe the company was a little overcautious, but what emerged from this tentative approach was a solid telecommuting policy that stands out as a model for other companies to emulate.

In the course of those two six-month trials, involving more than 100 employees, Bell Atlantic executives had ample opportunity to see both how telecommuting could *hurt* the telecommunications and how it could *help*.

"In the beginning we recruited a hundred people at one of our offices in Virginia, just to see how things would go," says telecommuting manager Bonnie High. "In the second pilot, we expanded the idea to include multiple work locations. We wanted to focus on what would happen if a number of people worked at several locations."

Bell Atlantic has offices all over Virginia, Maryland, Delaware, Pennsylvania, and New Jersey. It's a huge region. Consequently, the second pilot was a vast undertaking, with terrific potential for world-class screwups. Surprisingly, at least to some executives, both pilots went beautifully. Now the program is open to 16,000 management employees in the Bell Atlantic service area. High credits the company's cautious approach with winning converts.

"It's wiser to develop a policy and guidelines carefully, because then you have something upon which everyone can hang their hat," Bonnie High says. "The program is destined for success rather than failure. On the other hand, if you haphazardly introduce a program, you're going to upset a lot of people, have spotty implementation, and get all kinds of people frustrated."

As the pilot programs ended, Bell Atlantic was able to see clearly the many advantages of work-at-home arrangements. Other companies report similar experiences. In short, remote work offers plenty of advantages for companies in general and managers in particular.

Here's what telecommuting can offer your company.

Increased Productivity

Hard as it is for some managers to believe, you might get more work done at home than you ever would in the office, even if you were chained to your cubicle. But don't take our word from it. Listen to a manager.

"Most of our supervisors thought their telecommuting employees were more productive," says Denise Cichon, Aetna senior human resources consultant. "The employees themselves reported they were more productive, mostly because they had fewer distractions and there were no other people around. They were really task-directed."

Carol Nolan, head of the telecommuting program at Pacific Bell, reports productivity gains of up to 20 percent. Similar increases are reported by Diane Bengston, director of human resources in the information systems department of the Travelers, and by Bell Atlantic's Bonnie High. In fact, in two specific cases at Bell Atlantic, worker output jumped 200 percent over the previous year.

In surveys across the country, the sentiment is much the same. Nationally, managers and supervisors report productivity increases of between 5 and 20 percent among most of their remote workers. At Illinois Bell, managers estimated the productivity of home-based workers increased a full 25 percent. A study of telecommuting at another telecommunications firm, US West, showed even more dramatic increases in worker output, to between 30 and 40 percent. And in a joint program run by AT&T and the state of Arizona, 80 percent of the supervisors said their work-at-home employees were more productive than they had been when they were in the office all the time.

Workers, of course, agree wholeheartedly. More than 80 percent of the employees in that AT&T-Arizona program said they were better able to meet their work objectives and managed their time more efficiently. More than 70 percent of the employees who volunteered for the Puget Sound Telecommuting Demonstration in Washington State said they had been able to crank out far more work on the days they spent at home. Most of the 160 AT&T managers who took part in an L.A.–based telecommuting project reported that working at home boosted their output, and 40 percent said their productivity was enhanced "a lot."

Telecommuting consultant Gil Gordon isn't surprised at the higher level of work produced by telecommuters. Gordon believes most companies see productivity boosts of between 15 and 25 percent. But that shouldn't come as a shock. Just look at who works at home.

Employees who are allowed to telecommute are almost always highly motivated, solid self-starters, and compulsive goal-setters, Gordon points out. Just wind them up and off they go. And when these big producers are allowed to make their own rules about how they perform, many are so grateful for their company's trust in them that they *really* jam. "In my experience, depending on the nature of the job, people usually produce more. At the very worst, they break even," says Gordon. "But it's rare that that's all they do."

Michael Dziak, a telecommuting consultant and the brains behind Telecommute Atlanta, a one-year project to reduce air pollution in the city, believes smart managers can usually tell in advance which employee is likely to be a good home-based worker. "He or she is the overachiever, the person who usually works well on his or her own, someone who is already trusted," Dziak says.

So if the boss is worried that your work will go straight to hell, point him or her in the direction of Pacific Bell, AT&T, JC Penney, or any of the other successful corporate telecommuting ventures. The bottom line is this: If you are a trustworthy, diligent worker, your supervisor may find that your home-based experiment will prove more similar to heaven on earth.

A Better Bottom Line

Pacific Bell's Carol Nolan, who often provides advice to other companies considering work-at-home programs, often sells the idea to managers in terms of "wiffums." Translation: What's in it for me? It's usually not too difficult to make a case for telecommuting, she says. But unless the idea has "a lot of good wiffums, they probably won't go for it."

She points to the example of one large West Coast company that was expanding and considering the need for more office space. "They were growing, but they didn't want to lease space," she says. The costs of such a lease, simply to house six employees, were astronomical—on the order of a half-million dollars a year. So the manager in charge of the expansion came up with an idea: Let those six employees work at home. "The people he was working with were salespeople, so they already spent a lot of time out of the office, on the road, and they had laptop computers," says Nolan. In one bold stroke this risk-taking manager saved his company a half-million dollars.

Overhead costs were also of concern to management at US West, according to a study by CUNY telecommuting expert Kathleen Christensen. By instituting a telecommuting program, Christensen states, the company found that it could house six employees who worked at home part time, on a rotating schedule, in a space formerly used by four full-time, in-house employees.

Consultant Gil Gordon agrees that telecommuting can save companies money normally spent to house workers. "The long-term trend in downtown office space is that it will remain exceedingly expensive," he says. "It makes sense that if you can move those human beings out of downtown office space into a suburban office, as many companies are doing, you can cut the cost of office space by at least half. But if you move them into their own homes, you cut the cost of office space by 90 percent or more."

Bell Atlantic realizes cost savings of several hundred dollars a year per telecommuter as a result of office consolidation, says Bonnie High. But there are other bottom-line benefits, she points out. "In 1991, Bell Atlantic paid $48 million in disability costs," she explains. "With telecommuting I can identify several cases in particular in which our disability costs were lowered or eliminated. For example, we have one individual in middle-level management who has developed chronic fatigue syndrome. If he had not been offered the opportunity to work at home, we would have lost him to long-term disability, at a cost of more than $800,000 over a ten-year period. Instead, that individual is telecommuting, and the company has incurred zero expense. In another case, we had an employee who was undergoing chemotherapy. He was physically unable to commute. Now he's fully productive. Certainly the employee benefits from a health perspective, but the company also realized an estimated $30,000 cost savings [the estimated amount in disability payments to an unproductive worker]. Telecommuting for wellness is a grand opportunity for cost reduction."

Of course, a good deal of the illness that costs business money is not life-threatening, but rather consists of the common cold, intestinal bugs, and other garden-variety maladies. But companies that offer home as an alternative to the main office often find that their rate of absenteeism due to such minor illnesses drops. Employees who may not feel well enough to drive or take the train to work might feel up to working in their home office. They can dress comfortably, not have to worry about how they look, and cough, hack, wheeze, and sneeze to their heart's content without having to worry about spreading disease and contagion to others. And the same goes for employees who might miss work when their children are sick or when some other home or family crisis arises that requires immediate attention. Under those circumstances, though the worker might not get as much done as usual, there is usually still enough time to perform at least some tasks.

As Pacific Bell's Carol Nolan notes, we're not living in the 1950s anymore; families have changed. In most two-parent households, both parents hold jobs outside the home. Working parents require some recognition of that fact from their employers. "People need more flexibility in their lives," says Nolan. "Often workers take days off just to take care of problems in their personal lives, which costs the company in terms of absenteeism dollars. Whereas if you give people some flexibility with their schedules, then you have the capability of letting employees work at home, and they can deal more readily with whatever comes up."

Smarter Management (or, About Face)

Whenever the issue of home-based work rears its frightening little head among managers of the Stone Age variety, one complaint is often voiced: How will I know Jim (or John or Eileen or Denise) is working? These managers—you know who they are—put a lot of stock in a thing called "face time." When they can see your face, they know you're hard at work.

(What bosses like these probably *don't* know is, for all that time you spent on the telephone looking busy, you were really trying to get tickets to the Celtics-Lakers game. Or maybe, when Mr. or Ms. Big saw you tapping away furiously at your computer, he or she assumed you were working on your new proposal. But you were really typing out cover letters so you could find a new job where the boss wasn't as dense as fudge.)

There's nothing like telecommuting to show a company where its weak links are, and they're usually to be found among the ranks of resistant managers. Big surprise: The reason they resist is that they don't really know how to manage.

"I've heard just about every excuse in the book," says Carol Nolan. "But when they say no to telecommuting, what they're really saying is that they're not comfortable managing their employees. They're saying, 'I don't feel like I have the proper tools to manage my people, so I'm not gonna let them go.'

"I advised one group of managers that was really awful. One middle-level manager in particular said that telecommuting would never work in his section because 'we're a real team.' I said, 'That's a good point. But what happens when a member of the team gets sick? Or goes on vacation?' It was at that point that he knew I had caught him. His problem was that he just wasn't a very good manager. The truth was that he had some people who didn't work, who should have been put on disciplinary action, but he didn't have the guts to penalize them. I see this kind of thing in a lot of the companies I work with. As a society, we have not done a good enough job of choosing managers and giving them sound management skills."

Telecommuting often goads companies into taking a good look at how they, and their managers, run things. Inevitably, if they're really determined to get an honest answer, they come up against the age-old philosophy of "management by objective." The surest test of how well a company's supervisors are doing their job is how they manage workers who aren't physically in the office.

In many large companies, where employees may be spread out across the country in branch offices, management by objective probably won't come as such a shock. "Within Bell Atlantic, supervisors are really being placed in a situation of remote management more and more," says Bonnie High. "For example, I'm in a group where remote management is the norm. My supervisor is in Arlington, Virginia. I'm in Laurel, Maryland. Other employees in the group are in southern Maryland, New Jersey, and Pennsylvania. Co-location doesn't happen except when we have to get together for a staff meeting."

As companies become competitors in a global marketplace, opening up offices all over the world, it will become ever more important for managers to learn how to manage far-flung employees and to use the telecommunications tools that link everyone together. "People who rely on face-to-face meetings, who can't figure out ways to supplement that style with other ways of communicating and sharing information, just aren't going to succeed," says Lisa Volmar of Hayes Microcomputer in Atlanta. "The managers who walk by your desk, see you sitting there, and assume you are working aren't going to make it in this new environment. You can't manage people based on whether they show up at 8:30 and sit there until 5 or 6 and seem to stay busy."

It isn't uncommon, even in the best companies, for managers to worry about how they will be able to supervise these new invisible employees. "A lot of the managers here were concerned," says Diane Bengston of the Travelers. "They asked, 'How can I manage people like this? I'm not going to have anybody in the office.' But those concerns prove groundless. It all becomes manageable."

As supervisors and employees alike become used to the new

arrangement, most say they find that they communicate better. Expectations are expressed more clearly. Goals are set in mutual consultation.

"What happens is that managers begin to think more clearly about what they want done," says Joan Hope, work-family coordinator for First Union Bank in Charlotte, North Carolina. "They throw out their preconceptions about how they want to get to that point. [Telecommuting] opens up a dialogue between managers and employees about how they get things accomplished. They become more of a team."

Whether or not all managers see it, home-based work is part and parcel of a quiet revolution in the American workplace. As Daniel Dreyer puts it, "There's a definite shift going on in corporate America. The relationship between employee and employer is changing. It's no longer a 'parental' relationship; it's really more of a partnership."

Access to a Bigger Pool of Workers

As you'll recall, JC Penney started its highly successful telecommuting program among telemarketing clerks as a solution to two problems. One was the need to respond more flexibly to peak periods in catalog sales. Another was the desire to open up the labor market to people who might want to work but are unable to make the daily trek into the office.

Penney's needs employees who work seasonally, not employees who are looking for year-round, full-time employment. Young women with older parents living with them or newborns in the home fill the bill nicely. These workers represent an untapped resource.

But Penney's isn't the only company mining that resource. A company called SPAR/Burgoyne Marketing Services, which does market research in food stores, discount outlets, and drugstores, faced a pressing need back in the mid-1980s. It needed to reduce its data entry costs, which were running about $75,000 a month in late

1985. According to research by CUNY's Kathleen Christensen, SPAR executives figured it would be cheaper to farm out data entry to home-based operators than to do the work in-house. They were right. A year after the company inaugurated the home-based program, its data entry costs were down to $4,000 a month.

Now one way to look at it, as Christensen points out, is that the company stopped paying $14.13 an hour, on average, per worker. That figure includes the workers' pay, benefits, office space, electrical power, and equipment. The company then replaced the office-based workers with independent contractors who were paid less, received no benefits, and didn't take up office space. These new workers cost the company roughly $6.70 an hour per worker, representing a savings of $7.43 an hour.

How does this benefit workers? Many of the independent contractors are women with young children; they want to work but can't easily leave home to do it. These at-home positions allow them to earn money while enjoying a flexible schedule.

Christensen says the benefits to management are obvious: lower costs and decreased turnover. But for the workers there may be benefits to what, at first blush, seems like a wholly lopsided arrangement. Many of the independent contractors are women who have young children and who want to work but can't easily leave home to do it. Lack of job security and no benefits may be a high price to pay, but working at home gives them an opportunity they might not have otherwise.

Good Vibrations

Donelle Glatz, who was working for Crestar Bank in Richmond, Virginia, when she learned she was pregnant, says that if her company had been unable to accommodate her, she probably would have had to resign. Like many other telecommuters, she was a highly valued employee, so her supervisor at Crestar made an extra effort to keep her on board. As a result, Donelle was a happy employee. How much is one employee's happiness worth?

Why Your Boss Should Like Home-Based Work

- More productive workers—happier workers who have fewer interruptions get more done.
- More effective management—managing people from a distance often results in better communication, clear and mutual work objectives, and, overall, more efficient use of time and resources.
- Less absenteeism—a minor illness, the need to care for a sick relative, or personal business doesn't always have to mean a whole day missed when working from home.
- Reduced overhead—true if having employees work from home means saving on office space.
- Enhanced ability to attract new employees—companies that offer worksite flexibility are quite simply more desirable places to work.
- Cheaper and easier compliance with federal air quality regulations—companies that must comply find telecommuting a more effective and easier way to get workers off the road than company-sponsored vans and car pools.
- More loyal and motivated employees—workers who have some control over their work schedules and environment like their jobs more and better appreciate their employers.

To management, a happy employee is one who is more likely to stay and to radiate those good vibrations within and without the company. Home-based work has immeasurable value as a recruitment and retention tool. If a manager is faced with the potential loss of a star employee, there are really only two choices: let her go or figure out a way for her to stay. On balance, keeping a valued employee is cheaper than having to go out and hire and train a new one. There's a lot of experience tied up in a worker like Donelle, who had worked for her company for several years before faced with the possibility of separation. A good manager would have to wonder how long it would be before her replacement would know as much about the job as Donelle did.

"From a corporate perspective, home-based work offers Bell Atlantic an opportunity to attract and retain quality employees," says Bonnie High. "Simply because we offer a lot of work options, we've been cited by *Working Woman* magazine as one of the top 100 companies to work for. To the extent that a corporation can position itself as a favorable company to work for, it attracts and keeps quality employees."

Luring and retaining high-quality employees is very much at the heart of Pacific Bell's telecommuting program. "Companies do have an interest in making sure they stay competitive in the job market," says Carol Nolan. "We don't want to lose valued employees to other companies in the telecommunications industry. And from a practical point of view, we would rather not have to constantly train people. We try to instill a sense of loyalty in our professional staff, and we work very hard to keep those people employed with us."

Companies shouldn't make the mistake of assuming employees don't need or appreciate VIP treatment. They also ought to give some thought to the value of positive public relations. Money can't buy that kind of goodwill. Take, for example, Jeanne Eaker, the product support consultant for First Union, who has been working at home since August 1991 and loving virtually every minute of it. She hasn't forgotten who made it all possible.

"I had always given my best to my company, and I continue to do that," she says. In return for the company's willingness to accommodate her personal and family needs, she says, it gets her loyalty and commitment. "This is a wonderful place to work," she says. "The company is committed to making this a good environment for its employees, and the employees spread the word. That is one of the best things a company could have: word of mouth."

How One Company Does It

The Orange County facility of the computer company UNISYS is one of many California businesses that have enacted telecommuting programs. What you see here is an example of typical corporate telecommuting guidelines, courtesy of UNISYS. Note that these guidelines are specific to UNISYS Orange County and not to the company as a whole.

UNISYS Orange County Telecommuting Guidelines

- Telecommuting is a management option, not an employee benefit.
- Employees' salaries and benefits will not be changed as a result of their participation in the telecommuting program.
- All telecommuters must have prior written approval of their managers. Employees will be selected based on the suitability of their jobs, an evaluation of the likelihood of their being successful telecommuters, and an evaluation of their supervisors' ability to manage remote workers. Each department will make its own selections. Final approval may be reserved at the Directors' level.
- Managers and formal participants will sign the "Telecommuter's Agreement." This agreement details the responsibilities of the company and employee.
- If equipment is provided by UNISYS, the department will provide repairs. If employees use their own equipment, their department will help pay for a percentage of repairs, based on the amount of time an employee telecommutes. This will be reviewed on a case-by-case basis.

- Telecommuting telephone charges will be paid by the telecommuter's organization at UNISYS.
- All telecommuters and their managers will participate in studies to evaluate the effectiveness of the program.
- Employees can work at home up to a maximum of three days in a given week. Managers may limit or expand telecommuting further if they feel it is necessary.
- Telecommuters will be required to work a schedule agreed upon with their manager. They will also have to follow any guidelines set for communications, such as making regular calls to the voice mail system to check for messages.
- Employees will be required to designate a work area within their homes. This work area will be considered an extension of the employee's work area on UNISYS premises, and so the company's liability for injuries will also extend to this space. Employees will be responsible for maintaining safe conditions in their work area. The company's liability for injuries taking place while working at home will be confined to this area. The company's liability will also be confined to injuries taking place during the work hours agreed upon by the employee and his or her manager.
- Managers have the right to terminate a telecommuting arrangement made with an employee if the organization's needs are not being met. Employees who no longer wish to telecommute may also terminate their telecommuting arrangements and return to full-time in-office work at any time.

Reprinted with permission of UNISYS Orange County.

CHAPTER 4

WHY THEY MIGHT SAY NO—AND HOW TO GET THEM TO SAY YES

I once interviewed for an editorial position in Washington, D.C., while living in Philadelphia. The interview went very well, and the job sounded fun and challenging—another *new* magazine—but I wasn't sure it was worth the inconvenience of either a daily six-hour round-trip commute or setting up housekeeping in an efficiency and returning home on the weekends. I knew a couple of people who did that and worse. And I was absolutely not going to uproot my family again. We were taking our cue from humorist Lew Grizzard, author of *When I Get Back to Georgia, I'm Going to Nail My Feet to the Ground.* We were going to set ourselves down in one place and try not to budge.

A few days after the interview, the deputy executive director called to offer me the job. With no prompting whatsoever from me, he offered to let me work at home two days a week. Suddenly the job looked doable, and I said yes. *Carpe diem!* (That's Latin for either "Seize the day" or "Ten cents a fish." I'm never sure which.)

If something like this happens to you, consider yourself *extremely* lucky. In my interviews with countless home-based workers and their employers, I've seen very few examples of such open-mindedness. That's not to say such agreements aren't negotiated, but most experts concur that these are not routine occurrences. Far more likely, they say, is a home-based relationship negotiated sometime *after* you have been on the job and have had time to impress your boss with your verve, éclat, and savoir faire.

Let's suppose you've been on the job for more than a year. The supervisor knows and trusts you, respects your work, and appreciates your sense of initiative. You're a highly rated and presumably valued employee. Regardless, many bosses are going to need a good deal of convincing before they agree to take a chance on an idea that might seem unnatural to them.

You could gradually ease into a home-based work relationship, as some people do. Bell Atlantic telecommuting manager Bonnie High refers to this tactic as "guerrilla telecommuting." Start out by telling your supervisor that you need quiet time to complete an important project, and ask if you can take it home. After you've done this a few times, your boss may get used to the idea and just accept that there are some things you do better on your own.

"Suppose you work in purchasing and you're going to buy a dozen products, but you have 16 different proposals," explains Atlanta telecommuting consultant Michael Dziak. "Explain to your boss that you need time to go through all the proposals, and ask if it would be all right if you worked on them at home—without interjecting that you intend to do it again. If you do it and the boss is satisfied, you've planted the seed in his or her mind that it's OK to do it. A month or two later, another project comes up. Ask to do it again. Ease them into it."

What follows, then, is advice from some of the experts on how to make your best case for home-based flexibility. (Also see *Why Your Boss Should Like Home-Based Work* in Chapter 3.)

The Top Five Reasons Bosses Resist Home-Based Work

(and any other flexible work arrangement that makes sense)

Bosses can be supremely conservative. Some of them make Rush Limbaugh look like a sex-crazed dope fiend by comparison, or even a Boston Democrat. And when they resist change, they resist it with a gritty, hardheaded determination unmatched by the most recalcitrant of bulls.

In 1991 the Conference Board assembled a panel of corporate work-family executives to identify the barriers to flexible work arrangements, including telecommuting. Here are the top five reasons why bosses are inclined to say no to a more flexible workplace:

Supervision issues. They don't think they can manage invisible employees.

Lack of senior management support. If the supervisor cuts you some slack, someone else is going to cut her off at the knees.

Problems in administering benefits. Not so much of a concern for telecommuters who continue to work a full-time schedule, even if they're home part of the time. More a concern for arrangements like job sharing.

Concerns about customer needs. Will the customer be able to track you down at home? Will you respond quickly to the customer's request for service? (Or will it have to wait until you're back in the office?)

Head count. Again, this is more of a concern for other flexible staffing practices such as job sharing and phased retirement. How is the employee "counted" if he or she is only on the job a few hours a day or a few days a week? Is the employee full time or part time? And so on.

Reprinted with permission from *Work-Family Roundtable,* The Conference Board, December 1991.

Put Business First

Duncan Dieterly is an industrial psychologist for Southern California Edison, a nine-year employee and a supervisor in his company's disability rehabilitation program. It's his responsibility to help disabled employees return to work. He also helped Edison start its pilot telecommuting program. "As an industrial psychologist, I've been interested in telecommuting for about 15 years," he says. "We started our pilot at Edison in August 1991, and I was responsible for developing evaluative tools for that program." Dieterly himself started telecommuting in October 1991, working out of his home in Moreno Valley a couple of days a week. Working at home translated into more productive hours of work, since Dieterly didn't have to face the 56-mile commute into the office in Los Angeles. "In L.A. traffic, that translates into an hour-and-a-half to two-and-a-half-hour drive one way," he says.

As one of the pioneers at his company, Dieterly has had ample opportunity to observe the winning strategies that led to the establishment of Edison's telecommuting program. No one had to convince him of the benefits to the worker—but someone had to persuade upper-level management that home-based work could be beneficial to Southern California Edison.

In the last chapter, you'll recall, I outlined a broad range of potential telecommuting benefits: improved employee morale, corporate public image-building, and enhanced productivity. These are all important benefits, and perhaps managers will come to value them in time. But if you want to sell home-based work as an option for your company, steer clear of the "soft" sell—the contented employee argument, for example—and focus instead on the hard sell. Make your main selling point something that will seem directly beneficial to the firm. Incorporate the other, softer benefits into your pitch, but make sure you lead off with plenty of "wiffums" (what's in it for me?), as Carol Nolan of Pacific Bell calls them.

In his experience, Dieterly found company managers most receptive to those selling points that seemed immediately helpful or useful to them. "Focus on any strategy that's more businessy," he advises. "Human resources people like to talk about morale and productivity, and those are very important, but to many managers they are just minor issues."

Be prepared to document the ways in which having employees based at home improves the bottom line. Maybe having X number of workers operating out of their homes reduces the need for office space, as I've mentioned. Also, many companies now face the need to comply with federal clean air rules by reducing the number of vehicle miles traveled by employees to and from work. Companies that fail to comply with the law may face stiff fines, so telecommuting helps the employer achieve a significant bottom-line objective and avoid trouble with the feds.

At Bell Atlantic, where the telecommuting program has become somewhat more formalized, employees who hope to work at home have to spell out exactly what they expect to do there—and even more. "They have to identify a business problem that is solved by their working at home," says Bonnie High. "They have to do a cost-benefit analysis."

SIX EFFECTIVE TACTICS FOR OVERCOMING BOSSES' RESISTANCE

Reluctant as they are to do anything different or unusual—heaven forfend!—supervisors *can* be moved, according to the Conference Board panel. The panel rated the following tactics very effective in overcoming resistance to tearing down the barriers (assuming your company as a whole is committed to workplace flexibility):

Define flexibility as a business need. Sell the boss on the ways in which flexibility can actually help, not hinder, business.

Give managers increased authority. This perhaps speaks for itself. But companies that say they believe in flexibility have to be willing to allow their supervisors some leeway in promoting more liberal schedules.

Relate to productivity. Provide evidence to managers that flexibility increases the amount of work that is done. As we saw in Chapter 1, there's very little question about whether home-based employees maintain productivity.

Document employee needs. Show the manager how flexible work practices respond to such problems as middle-aged employees with ailing parents to care for. Again, this may not be as impressive as pointing out the possible cost savings in office rentals, but every little bit helps.

Develop and distribute guidelines. Managers feel more secure if everything is spelled out in a memo.

Use information on competitors' programs. If it works for those nincompoops at Cogsworth Cogs, it's just gotta work for us here at Spacely Sprockets.

Reprinted with permission from *Work-Family Roundtable,* The Conference Board, December 1991.

Some business benefits are fairly obvious. Traveling salesmen, for example, have worked from home for years. Not going into the office puts them closer to their clients.

Take, for example, Cheri Shore, a manufacturing representative and systems design consultant for Pacific Bell. Until a few years ago, she reported to the main office in Los Angeles, driving into town from suburban Altadena. Now she works from home almost every day, reporting into the main office about once every two weeks. As a systems design consultant, Cheri has one very important customer—the world-famous Jet Propulsion Laboratories—which, as it happens, is just a little over a mile from her home.

"I spend a lot of my time out at JPL," says Cheri, whose husband, Bob Grenader, is a home-based manufacturer's representative selling computer equipment. "I work in an environment where you're supposed to be out with your customers, making sure they know what services we can offer to solve their problems. That's the nature of my job. I don't have anybody reporting to me. I manage my own time.

"When I was assigned to JPL, I laughingly told everybody that one of my goals was to become so well positioned with this customer that they wouldn't be sure whose payroll I was on. In order to do that, I'd just about have to live with them. It kind of developed from there."

For the most part, Cheri controls her own schedule, rolling out of bed at 7 A.M. and spending the rest of the day either at home or out at JPL. "The unspoken agreement is that between 8:30 and 5 I'm on company time," she says. "Whether I'm here or at home is anybody's guess. The only way to get hold of me is by pager." For Cheri's supervisor, the benefit of this long-distance arrangement is obvious. Good relations with a major customer—JPL employs between 8,000 and 9,000 people—is always in a company's best interests. Says Cheri, "No one has ever challenged me on this."

Be prepared for a formidable challenge if your reasons for working at home are somewhat frivolous. If you want the boss to agree to your proposal, says CUNY telecommuting expert Kathleen Christensen, offer appropriate reasons, not just that it seems like a swell idea or that it's the only way you'll ever get all your laundry done.

FLEXIBLE ALTERNATIVES

You can't always get what you want. But if you try sometimes, you get what you need.

Perhaps your main concern is flexibility, but you don't need—or can't get—the level of flexibility afforded by home-based work. There are a number of alternatives worth considering, ones that many industries find more acceptable. You might find, too, that as companies begin to get used to these rather restrained experiments, they become more willing to try out telecommuting. Think of these intermediate steps as the thin edge of the wedge. Here are some of the more common flexible work practices, according to a survey by the Conference Board:

Permanent part-time work. This is a slimmed-down schedule—20 or 30 hours a week instead of the usual 40. A new wrinkle on this is the "school day schedule," in which workers are allowed to leave the office in time to get home to care for their school-age children. Frequently these part-time positions offer reduced or no benefits. Ninety percent of the companies surveyed offered regular part-time work.

Flextime. Fifty percent of the firms surveyed offered this option, a schedule in which employees are allowed to choose flexible starting and quitting times as long as they work the standard 40 hours.

Compressed workweek. Known in some companies as a 4-10 program (meaning four ten-hour days a week), this option was offered by 36 percent of the surveyed companies. Participating employees are permitted to work four extra-long days, with three days off instead of the usual two.

Job sharing. Two people divide the responsibilities of one normally full-time position, drawing salary and benefits commensurate with the time each works. Only 22 percent of the surveyed firms provide this alternative.

Source: *Flexible Staffing and Scheduling in U.S. Corporations,* Research Bulletin No. 240, 1989, The Conference Board, Inc.

Go Slowly

Once you've got a receptive audience—i.e., a supervisor willing to listen—the next step is to propose a small-scale experiment. Never expect your supervisor, or your company as a whole, to leap into home-based work. More likely they'll want to move slowly.

Wendell Joice is a personnel research psychologist and project manager in the federal Office of Personnel Management. In early 1993, OPM's cooperative venture with other federal agencies—the so-called Flexiplace program—was just making the transition from the small pilot demonstration to a more broad-based program. OPM became involved in the Flexiplace program in 1989.

Joice had been telecommuting informally before 1989, but with his agency's support he began researching home-based work as a way to recruit and retain the best people. Since Flexiplace began, Joice has worked from his home near Walter Reed Hospital practically every day, on a split shift. "I like coming to work in the morning, and at noon I go home and work there the rest of the day. I live close enough to the office that that's not a problem," he says.

Flexiplace started small, giving program organizers an opportunity to try many different ideas and see what worked best for both home-based workers and their supervisors. "Don't go in to the manager with a rigid plan, full of elaborate reporting requirements and so on," Joice suggests, based on his experience. "That will just cause alarm."

When you start a home-based work program, it's important to communicate as clearly as possible with company managers about what's going on. Many companies, Bell Atlantic included, sponsor in-house training to explain to supervisors how the program is going to work and provide useful tips on how to manage by remote control. "The objective there is to teach supervisors to manage by performance and not by observation," says Bonnie High. "As a supervisor, you're probably kidding yourself if you think someone is busy just by looking at them. They could be sitting there writing a grocery list when they're supposed to be writing a report."

How to Manage the Home-Based Worker

Many of the nation's most successful telecommuting programs offer their managers training to help them become more comfortable and effective at managing remote-control underlings. Here are some of the best tips, drawn from the experience of companies such as Pacific Bell, GTE, the Travelers, and others:

Spell out your expectations. Tell the telecommuter exactly what you want him or her to accomplish. State clearly, and in writing, how the employee's work will be reviewed and rewarded. And remember, a handshake is never an adequate substitute for a clearly detailed written agreement.

Review employee progress. An every-once-in-a-while, as-long-as-you're-here, oh-I-just-remembered system of employee review is never appropriate, even when your workers are always in the office. But when they are *out* of the office, it is imperative that you formalize the review process and keep track of it on a frequent, regular basis.

Keep in touch. Understand that one of the pitfalls of telecommuting is isolation. If you're normally the type of manager who supervises at arm's length, this is a good opportunity for you to develop better communications skills. Don't leave the home-based worker to drift. This does *not* mean that you should be on the phone to your employee so often that he or she might just as well be in the office. Communicate too much, or too often, and the employee may begin to wonder whether he or she is really trusted. Also require the employee to report to the office for important meetings, and perhaps even special occasions like a farewell lunch for the office manager.

Pay attention to workers who remain office-bound. Phillip Mahfood, in *Homework: How to Hire, Manage and Monitor Employees Who Work at Home* (Probus Publishing Co., 1992), recommends that you remain keyed in to the needs of your office staff, who may not actively support telecommuting or the telecommuters if they feel they are being ignored.

Support the telecommuter's choice. If home-based workers suspect you're conspiring to do them in, the experiment is bound to fail. Telecommuters needs to know that you're behind them.

Get It in Writing

While you don't want to have *too* many rules, it is important—both for your supervisor's sake and your own—to have some. You should try to spell out at least a few of the conditions that you will be governed by. As much as possible, these conditions should cut both ways. That is, they should make your boss feel safe, but they should help you to feel comfortable, too. At first you may find that these agreements tend to be weighted somewhat more in favor of your supervisor. Pacific Bell's Carol Nolan says, "I believe that, as time goes on, managers become more and more comfortable with home-based employees. But in the beginning, you have to bend over backward."

Again, the goal is to make your manager feel more secure in the arrangement. One of the supervisor's deepest fears, as we mentioned previously, is the issue of "face time." Since he or she is not going to see you, you're going to have to provide some other means of accountability. So clearly you need to reassure your supervisor that you are working.

One of the benefits of working at home is that you can work at your own pace, on your own schedule. Some people, as we've seen, work at a blistering pace for five hours and then take the rest of the day to attend to other concerns, such as Little League practice or driving Mom to the dialysis clinic. Others work in blocks, taking a few hours off here and there and working at odd times—nights and weekends, for instance. But regardless of your personal schedule, you ought to agree in writing to be available during a particular block of time every day. Of course, your supervisor could insist that you *always* be available. But many bosses aren't as hard-nosed about it and will agree to a smaller block. Your employer may also be reassured if you agree to be available by pager, as Pacific Bell's Cheri Shore is.

Some managers are governed by a time-clock mentality, so blocking out a schedule will be reassuring to them. But others are more impressed by the work you do than by how much time you spend sitting at your desk, staring at your computer. The most important sign that you are working is that you actually complete your work. For this reason, in addition to blocking out a schedule you should work with your manager to agree on the work you are expected to accomplish on the days you work from home. Give your boss some means to measure your progress, a way of tracking your work. "You and your manager have to be very explicit about what your 'products' are and what are the benchmarks against which your progress will be measured," says CUNY's Kathleen Christensen.

A few examples of benchmarks:

- If you're a data entry clerk, you will input X number of forms during the day.
- If you write technical reports, you must commit to completing a specific number of pages or chapters.
- If you are a sales representative, you must contact at least as many prospects in your at-home position as you do now in the office—preferably more.

Some workers have specific tasks that must be completed on a timely basis. But most home-based workers, says consultant Michael Dziak, are "knowledge workers." It's harder to specify daily goals for employees who are pursuing long-term projects. So make sure you and your boss break down such projects into measurable chunks, setting periodic goals or benchmarks—like agreeing to come up with a launch plan for your new environmental law journal by May 1, next year's business plan by June 1, questions for focus groups by July 1, and so on.

"You must go home with a 'deliverable,'" says Dziak. That is, agree beforehand on a specific work objective that you are expected to accomplish when you are home. When you return to work, sit down with your boss and review your progress. In Dziak's experience, many supervisors who learn to set objectives for their telecommuters become better managers of *all* their employees. Perhaps for the first time, he says, "communication suddenly increases between the workers and their manager."

Many firms, such as Pacific Bell and Bell Atlantic, require workers and managers to sign joint telecommuting agreements, spelling out work objectives in the clearest possible terms. Dziak and other experts recommend that you try to obtain copies of other companies' home-based work agreements to use as models for your own.

Tina Koyama of Seattle Metro hammered out an agreement with her supervisor before she began working at home as a newsletter editor. "His main concerns were that I meet with him the day before I worked at home to tell him what I planned to accomplish," she says. "The day after, I would return to work and report to him on what I had done. A few months into the arrangement, we had developed such a rhythm that I didn't have to worry about consulting with him on such a regular basis. He knew I wasn't going to goof off."

Jeanne Eaker, the First Union Bank product support consultant, made similar arrangements with her immediate supervisor. "Every other week we sat down and had a meeting and went over project sheets, going into great detail about what I was doing at home," says Jeanne. "It was my responsibility to keep him informed at all times. I also kept a log of the time I worked at home and what I worked on."

Flo Phillips, First Union personnel director, believes that in time managers do become accustomed to not seeing your face. "What happens is, they begin to think more carefully about what needs to be done," she says. "They throw out their preconceptions about how to get to that point. When corporations telecommute, they open up a dialogue between managers and employees about work. Employees and supervisors become more of a team in getting things done."

There's another reason why you don't want to commit to

telecommuting on the strength of a handshake alone. When you put things in writing, both you and your supervisor minimize the chances of miscommunication. One of the main reasons people want to work at home, says CUNY's Kathleen Christensen, is the opportunity to set their own work hours. But she knows of one very loose telecommuting agreement that went sour pretty quickly, simply because the boss expected that the telecommuting employee in question was going to continue to work exactly the same hours as when she was in the office. That wasn't what the telecommuter had in mind, but then again, she had never spelled it out. It was the telecommuter's intention to work eight hours a day, but not necessarily the same eight hours as everyone else. Consequently, every time her supervisor called—and the employee was not at her desk—the boss jumped to the conclusion that she was not really working.

"Logically, for bosses it's a very short leap from 'Oh, he's not here' to 'Oh, he's not working,'" says Christensen. "The boss has to have some understanding as to when the employee is going to be available."

Agree to Keep in Touch

Some bosses like to chat on the phone. Others go for the strictly impersonal touch of computerized communication via E-mail. Some want you to "be there" at a certain time during the day, in case they need to confer with you, while others will be happy if you just remember to check in with them once a day.

Be Flexible

Suppose Tuesdays and Thursdays are your work-at-home days, and the Executive Vice President In Charge Of Long Memos schedules a meeting for next Tuesday. You could whine and say, "But I'm supposed to be *hoooome* that day...." Too bad. As part of your telecommuting agreement, you should acknowledge that you will need to attend major corporate events, even if they inconveniently fall on the days when you are usually working at home.

At the same time, getting it in writing sends a very clear message to your supervisor that, although you intend to honor your commitment to attend important functions, he or she shouldn't just call you in for trivial things.

Be Prepared to Make Concessions

Some companies, such as Bell Atlantic, expect home-based employees to bear the cost of equipment. "We believe that home-based work is a dual investment for a dual return," says Bonnie High. "Both the company and the employee benefit, so we believe both should have some 'skin' in the game. Bell Atlantic provides telephone lines into the home. We also provide special services on the line. But after that, it's up to the employee to provide all the other necessary equipment."

Don't Force the Issue

Whatever the specific details of your agreement, one provision is essential: Make it clear that either you or your employer can opt out of the arrangement at any time. In a broader sense, if you manage to get your employer interested in piloting a home-based work program, ask him or her to let supervisors decide for themselves whether they want to become involved. No one should be required to take part in the program. That's one sure way to guarantee failure.

"You have to make telecommuting easy for the manager to get into—and out of—so the manager can arrange it any way he or she likes," says Wendell Joice of the government's Office of Personnel Management. "You have to make the program reversible, so no one is locked in. If an employee isn't working out, the manager can call him or her back into the office. You want to make the manager feel safe in making this behavior change. And don't force managers who are against it into the program. If you force them, they'll fight it."

Conversations With Your Boss

You've decided to take the plunge and schedule that little talk with your boss. You want to work at home, and that's what you're going to say, but...how to say it? How will you counter the supervisor's objections?

Remember to stay focused on how your home-based venture benefits the company. If the supervisor goes for the idea, you, of course, will derive one of the most tangible benefits: a measure of freedom and self-determination you don't now enjoy. But don't sound apologetic. Don't approach your supervisor with the idea that he or she would be doing *you* a favor by letting you work at home. You're not a supplicant, so get off your knees.

Rather, approach this meeting from the point of view of a valued employee who has something worthwhile to offer the company. Try not to make the idea seem too revolutionary. Capitalists don't cotton to revolutions in the workplace. Don't get too dramatic, and don't overpromise. Stick to the facts, and drive home the benefits.

Imagine easing into a conversation that goes something like this:

You: I want to speak with you about an idea of mine, something that could help me but could also benefit the company.

The Big Cheese: Hmmmmm. (He looks dubious). Go on.

You: To get right to the point, I want to work at home one or two days a week. Working at home would give me a bit more control over how I do my work. It would get me out of a long, exhausting commute. I would be able to see more of my family. Those things are all important to me. But I've been doing my homework on this one, B.C., and I think there's something in this for the company too.

B.C.: Let me get this straight. You want to be out of the office for two days a week, and this is going to help the company?

You: Think about what your days are like, B.C. The phone rings all the time, someone's always knocking at your door, there are constant interruptions. My days are pretty much the same. Not all of those interruptions are necessary. You know that my job requires a good deal of concentration, and sometimes all those interruptions make it hard to concentrate. If I could take some of my work home—those parts of my job that require peace and quiet—I could do my job more effectively.

There's also the matter of the new federal air pollution laws. This company, along with all the others here in Center City, are under orders to reduce the amount of pollution caused by workers. That means getting cars off the road. You remember when we tried van pooling, B.C. It didn't last. It was expensive, and no one wanted to do it. If you allow some of us to work from home a day or two every week, the company might be able to meet the federal requirements in a way that workers will find acceptable, and all without having to spend enormous amounts of money.

Then there's the question of office space. In the last three years, we've added a dozen new analysts, but we never had room for more than three. We've doubled up on office space, but things are still jammed. Next year, the division is scheduled to expand. Send some of us home on a regular basis and you can relieve the pressure without having to spend a penny on additional office space.

B.C.: Sounds too good to be true.

You: That's what a lot of other companies said. That is, until they did it. I've taken the liberty of requesting documentation from Enormous Telephone Company, which started a work-at-home program five years ago, as well as a report prepared by the Extremely Conservative Highly Credible Business Research Organization.

Oh, and here's a news clipping from your favorite human resources journal, Controlling People Daily. It's about our competitor, Smokestack Industries. They just started a home-based work program for middle-level managers.

B.C.: Old Smokestack? Isn't this all a little gee-whiz for them?

You: Apparently not. And by all accounts, their productivity is up 25 percent in the departments where home-based work is an option.

B.C.: But we've never done this before. Besides, how would anyone ever know what you were up to?

You: True, we have never done this. I don't think we should leap into this with both feet. We should allow work-at-home arrangements on a trial basis, with a limited number of people at first. Let human resources manage it. Require that we all develop business plans showing precisely how our working at home fills a clear business need.

Leave it up to individual managers to decide whether they want to participate. And leave it up to the discretion of management to decide whether to call employees back into the office if things don't work out. Nothing's chiseled in stone.

Here, take a look at how the Wide Load Trucking Company does it. This is a copy of their model work-at-home agreement.

You raised a good question, too, about accountability. A lot of managers in the other companies where working at home is now an option worried about the same thing. For most of them, it was really a simple matter of communicating with their employees about what they were expected to do on their days home and checking in with them when they returned to the office. And in some jobs, like mine, it's simple to track progress. I have to contact 12 clients a day and prepare written reports for you on my progress. You ought to know fairly quickly whether I'm living up to my end of the agreement.

B.C.: Well, if it's good enough for Old Smokestack, it ought to be good enough for us. Let's talk about this some more and think about how we can make it happen.

This approach may work best for employees on an executive level, but for most of the rest of us, a more structured, definitive plan is in order. Depending on your corporate culture, it might be wise not to go it alone, particularly if you don't seem to be getting a receptive audience. Try to get the interest of your company's human resources manager. Note that what sometimes works best is a broad-based telecommuting policy that ultimately has the potential to benefit *many* employees, not just one—meaning you. One of the chief complaints about home-based work is the issue of fairness. In the long run, such gripes could undermine your right to work at home. It might be better to get together with like-minded employees—as the clerks in Cathy Kuehl's Minnesota government office did (see Chapter 1)—and work for a structured plan that provides more or less equal opportunity and flexibility for all.

TIPS FOR REMOTE-CONTROL MANAGEMENT

If your company is considering instituting a work-at-home option for its employees, it probably won't fly unless the managers and supervisors are signed on. Even then, expect some managers to resist with all their might. Whatever they do, company leaders should not require managers to support the program. Managers who are obliged to knuckle under will find ways to sabotage the effort. Far better to get them behind the idea. Here are some features of many of the most successful programs:

Management by objective. This is an old tried-and-true management practice, yet too many managers remain impressed by surface details. That is, does everybody *look* busy? As we know, appearances can be deceiving. Managers should learn to set goals, and deadlines for achieving them. They ought to be encouraged to meet on a regular basis with telecommuters—and, indeed, all employees under their supervision—to review job objectives and to make sure the work remains on track.

Commitment in writing. Ask that both the managers and the managed put their objectives in writing. This gives everybody easily measurable benchmarks. Managers are mainly concerned about the issue of trust, as an article in the human resources journal *Training* (May 1992) points out. But as writer Bob Filipczak notes, "If managers can verify that employees are producing results, there's no need to worry much about 'trust.'"

Leadership by example. Some of your managers are going to be more open-minded than others and will likely have good things to say about telecommuting. They should be enlisted to help sell the idea to the doubting Thomases and Thomasinas. At the Travelers, the human resources department keeps records of managers and supervisors who have taken part in its workplace flexibility program so that they in turn can provide support to other managers who are experiencing difficulties.

Proof that telecommuting meets important corporate needs. Companies need to be competitive not just in their products or services but also in their corporate image and their ability to maintain a quality work force. Give managers proof that telecommuting has helped other companies—especially competitors—recruit and retain valued employees. Provide evidence that telecommuting enhances productivity. Demonstrate how the company benefits from workplace flexibility.

Rewards for managers who exercise good telecommuting management skills. If a work-at-home program really is a corporate priority, supervisors must know that not only will they not be penalized for participating in such a program, but they will be appropriately rewarded.

Top management that visibly supports the program. If your company is really only paying lip service to telecommuting, count on your managers to get that message, too. As Vivian Jarcho, program manager of work life and family issues for the Department of Justice, commented in a survey of top work-family managers: "The visible support of the former attorney general and other department leaders has been a significant factor leading to further development of flexible work arrangements as part of our work life strategy."

Not too many rules. Commenting in the same survey, Al Bergerson, director of personnel policy development for Eastman Kodak, wrote, "We have not encumbered supervisors with overly restrictive guidelines for approving flexible work arrangements. We have put the responsibility in the supervisor's hands. Our success is the result of the framework and general parameters of the policy, and the degree of authority given to supervisors to approve requests. We leave it to the respective supervisor and employee to work out an arrangement that will work for them and not adversely affect their business goals."

Meeting the Company Halfway

Suppose you do your homework and draw up a dazzling presentation on the merits of telecommuting, and the company still says no. What then?

You could give up altogether. You could reassess your personal needs and try proposing another flexible work arrangement. (See *Flexible Alternatives* in this chapter.) But there is one new option on the horizon that has already undergone some testing, mostly in the smog-choked cities of southern California. It's sort of a halfway point between home and work, and it often proves more palatable to management than work-at-home proposals. It's called the telecommuting center.

A telecommuting center is a conventional workplace in most respects. It looks like a downtown office, with 10 or 20 brightly colored workstations and cubicles, full telephone service, computers, printers, fax machines, conference rooms, and secretarial service. The main difference—perhaps the only difference that counts—is that it is close to where workers live. From the perspective of big business, it seems a far more conventional workplace than does a converted second bedroom or den. What's more, one telecommuting center may house employees from several different businesses. So instead of having to get up early and drive into Los Angeles, for example, workers can sleep in a little bit and drive only a few miles to a telecommuting center closer to their home.

Telecommuting centers are well known—and well received—throughout Europe. The concept has been slower to catch on here in the United States, where it's confined largely to pilot projects in California, Hawaii, and Washington State. For the most part, these experimental centers are jointly funded and operated by state and local governments and local businesses.

One multimillion-dollar pilot program now under way, overseen by transportation specialists at the University of California, should lead to the opening of as many as 12 pilot telecommuting centers in three heavily congested areas of southern California: Orange County,

Sacramento, and San Diego. David Fleming of UC-Davis is the program manager.

By June 1994, Fleming predicts that telecommuting centers will be sprouting up all over the suburban landscape, in existing office buildings, storefronts, and even strip shopping centers. One such center is already in operation near UC-Davis. "In my neighborhood the telework center occupies the second floor of a shopping center," Fleming says. "It's full of offices." Over time, he believes large businesses will help to subsidize these local telecommuting centers through a system of graduated rent, easing the financial strain in the early going, then rising as the benefits become more apparent to the companies and the need for expensive big-city office space drops. Eventually, he thinks, government will be able to eliminate subsidies altogether, as businesses take over the day-to-day operation of these centers. "I don't think they should be totally subsidized," he says. "But for the moment, the carrot has to be held out there."

Participating businesses will attempt to divert many of their employees into these centers, Fleming says, which presumably will be close to where they live. "We are targeting workers who can walk or ride their bikes to the center," he says.

Though telecommuting centers sound like an ideal option for companies skittish about letting their employees take off for home two or three days a week, Fleming understands that there are obstacles. Business leaders are, by nature, conservative, and they view any new wrinkle with some suspicion. It has not escaped his notice that similar experiments, including one in Washington State, folded when government support ended. Businesses may be mostly concerned, Fleming says, that telecommuting centers will lead to decentralization. But, he adds, plenty of companies already manage employees in distant branch offices. Bradford Hesse, co-director of the Center for Research on Technology, notes, for example, that Apple Computer of Cupertino, California, has already transferred production facilities—and workers—to Texas, where they are "just an electronic mail message away from staying in touch with each other in spite of the distance." As Fleming says, "Decentralization is already happening."

Fleming is also encouraged by the success of other projects, such as the Teleport Telecenter for employees who work in the high-tech industries of Silicon Valley. Those workers often face commutes as long as an hour and a half one way. The Teleport Telecenter, on the fringes of the valley, is generating considerable official interest. "They have local government behind it like mad," Fleming says, adding that so far it is receiving encouraging reviews.

Fleming and his colleagues at UC-Davis are pushing telecommuting with apostolic fervor. "What we have is something that can reduce pollution, cut people's commutes, and improve the quality of life," he says. "It can benefit society, businesses, and employees. I like to think of my job as awakening people to the idea that this will work. This is a socially responsible way to improve the bottom line."

Chapter 5

Legal Entanglements

For most of us, a day in the home office is blissfully uncomplicated. Working at home is like an escape valve in the pressure cooker of work life. You can sleep in if you need to, start early and work late if you prefer, wear your comfy slippers, skip shaving, and have lunch with a friend at your favorite neighborhood deli.

But sometimes working at home may pose perplexing legal complications. Some of these are easily dealt with; others, not so. In this chapter I'll deal with a few of the most common potential legal pitfalls, such as taxes and local zoning.

Before I start, this disclaimer: I am *not* an attorney. So what follows is definitely not legal advice. For any and all legal concerns that you may have regarding telecommuting, I urge you to speak with your firm's solicitor or with your own attorney.

Employee or Hired Gun?

Some companies deal with the issue of work-at-home arrangements by reclassifying employees as consultants or independent contractors. In the past this was also a handy way of retaining the services of retired senior executives. From the employee perspective, free-agent status typically means forgoing benefits. It also means having to report and pay quarterly estimated taxes and Social Security. All of your income should be reported to the Internal Revenue Service on a 1099 form. This arrangement may be just fine for people who value their independence so much that they are willing to make certain sacrifices and who already have such benefits as health and dental coverage by virtue of an employed spouse—or who make enough money to pay for their own health and dental care. Employers like it, too, because eliminating a worker's benefits and reducing their payroll taxes saves money.

Should you take this route? Only you know the answer to that. If you don't mind some of the inconveniences we've talked about, go for it—though clearly you also sacrifice whatever job security you might have had as a full-time employee.

But bear in mind another potential risk. For the past few years, the IRS has been keeping tabs on company reports of 1099 wage earners. It's the agency's contention that some companies use independent contractors in a strategy to avoid paying payroll taxes on people who should properly be classified as employees. According to an article in *Personnel Journal* (October 1991), the feds lose $1.56 billion in revenue each year as a result of corporate efforts to disguise their so-called "invisible employees." In 1991, according to IRS spokesman Ellen Murphy, the agency performed 1,700 audits on firms nationwide, resulting in the reclassification of 90,000 workers, and collected almost $20 million in payroll taxes from companies. In one hugely sobering 1989 case, decided in U.S. claims court a year later, a company that was alleged to have misclassified its employees and independents was assessed a whopping fine of $11 million.

(The IRS is also concerned about independent contractors for another pretty good reason, says Murphy. The earnings of a substantial majority of these freelance workers—perhaps as many as 70 percent—are never reported to the federal government by their employers, and the workers themselves don't report their true earnings on their tax returns either. For fairly apparent reasons, the federal tax collectors frown on this kind of behavior.)

Obviously, if the IRS starts examining the tax records of your company, your arrangement—as they say in French—may be in deep *merde*.

When Is an Employee Really an Employee?

The answer just isn't all that clear. When IRS agents embark on a hunting expedition in search of misclassified employees, they typically audit a company's payroll records, with particular attention to the aforementioned 1099 forms. If they find records showing that more than $10,000 of a wage earner's reported 1099 income comes from that company, the work relationship between the company and its so-called consultant comes in for closer scrutiny.

However, an IRS investigation does not automatically mean you and your company are playing fast and loose with the tax code, Ellen Murphy says. In many instances the feds find such business relationships to be perfectly legit. Unfortunately for those of us who have a difficult time coping with ambiguity, the IRS makes its determinations on a case-by-case basis, so it is really quite impossible to give you a set of rules to follow. However, there are a few basic rules of thumb:

- Do you have other sources of income? If so, the firm that is your main source of income might be regarded as just another client, and you and the company could be in the clear.
- Do you have control over how you do your job? If you can work when and how you decide to, with little or no direction from the company, this may be taken as a sign of your independence. If, however, you work according to a rigidly enforced schedule, taking explicit directions from the company, and you work on company-provided equipment, the IRS may be less likely to look charitably upon you and the company in question.

- Does the company have people on the payroll who do approximately the same job you do? If so, the company could be in for a going-over. The IRS may quite legitimately ask what makes you—someone who does the same job as all the other paid, full-time employees—different. If there isn't much of a difference, your company may be in trouble.

That said, however, the IRS has examined certain cases in which the free agents in question have no other sources of income, take their marching orders from one company, and perform tasks remarkably similar to those of full-time employees—and, inexplicably, has decided there is no violation of the tax laws. "In most cases it's not really a close call," Murphy says, "but there are always situations where a person might be considered independent."

So if working independently is the only way you can get the freedom you want, consider such an arrangement very, very carefully.

The Home Office Deduction

Say you work for a small insurance company as a technical writer. On Mondays, Wednesdays, and Fridays you head into the main office in the city. But on Tuesdays and Thursdays, to give you quiet time to write newsletter copy without constant interruptions, the boss permits you to work at home.

In your little house in the suburbs, you have set aside a small spare bedroom for your office. In it sits a desk, and on the desk is a computer, a monitor, a printer, a modem, a separate dedicated phone line, and a small fax machine. At no time do you use the home office for anything but work for your employer. There are no Super Mario Bros. video games plugged into the computer. The closet, which begs to be stuffed with all your out-of-season clothes, is instead stacked high with boxes of paper, pens, spare printer cables, file folders, and legal pads. The only books on your shelf are dictionaries, a thesaurus, technical manuals, a style book, and the *New York Public*

Library Desk Reference. No Tom Clancy potboilers, no comic books. Everything in and about this room says work, work, and nothing but work.

Tax day rolls around, and you claim your Spartan accommodations as a deductible expense. A few months pass. And then one dark day comes that heart-stopping missive from your pals at the Internal Revenue Service. Congratulations! Your home office deduction has been disallowed, and you owe Uncle Sam. Prepare to open a vein.

I can't offer legal advice on your particular situation. But when it comes to the home office deduction, I can offer you a few rules of thumb that may save you an arm and a leg.

If you work for someone else—that is, if you are not, very strictly speaking, self-employed—you may have one heck of a time persuading the IRS that you are entitled to the home office deduction. More often than not, this deduction is reserved for those who work for themselves—and even then, the feds can be persnickety. Expect the Spanish Inquisition.

The IRS is typically pretty stingy about granting the home office deduction. After many years of sorry and unprofitable experience granting the deduction to people who only occasionally used their home office—or didn't use it for work—the IRS stepped up its enforcement efforts back in the 1980s. The agency took the view that in order for someone to be granted a deduction, the home office essentially had to be the sole place of business. In June 1991, the Fourth Circuit Court of Appeals liberalized that narrow definition, allowing the deduction for workers who spent "substantial time" in their home office—not necessarily 40 hours a week. That ruling also specified that in order to qualify for the deduction, workers must demonstrate that they had no other suitable place in which to perform their work.

So far, so good. In the case in question, Nader E. Soliman, a McLean, Virginia, anesthesiologist, claimed his right to the deduction. Though he worked for several hospitals, none provided him with an office. In order to handle correspondence, maintain patient records, or process bills, he argued, he was forced to use the office he had set up in a spare bedroom of his condo. The expenses for that office, he claimed, were deductible—even though he only spent about a third of his working hours there. The Circuit Court concurred.

But the Supreme Court didn't buy the anesthesiologist's argument. In an 8–1 ruling, the court said Soliman wasn't eligible for the deduction because he performs most of his actual work—putting people to sleep—outside his home. In order to qualify for the deduction, the court ruled, the home office really must be the "focal point" of a business.

Frankly, the Supreme Court's ruling defies explanation. As Bernadette Grey, editor of *Home Office Computing*, commented, the court's "focal point" test is illogical. She says, "That's like saying Burger King shouldn't be allowed to deduct the rent or mortgage of its corporate headquarters because the focal point of its activity is its restaurants."

THE HOME OFFICE LOWDOWN

One of the best articles on the subject of home office deductions, written in plain English, appeared in the September 1991 edition of a journal called *Management Accounting*. The article is entitled "Taxes: Home Office Deduction Eligibility," and it was written by Peter Barton and Clayton Sager. If you can't find it, ask your librarian to track it down for you.

Before you try putting your case to the test, consider this: A self-employed professional with a reasonable point of view and a legitimate need for a home office argued all the way to the Supreme Court, and he lost. If you are not self-employed and you have a perfectly good office in a downtown building, your chances of sweet-talking the IRS are about as good as Al Capone's. Russian roulette gives you better odds.

The best advice, particularly since it involves little or no risk, is not to go after the deduction unless you are an independent contractor doing most or all of your work at home. If in doubt, check with your accountant or attorney.

Incidentally, there is one other very important reason why the IRS might be loath to permit you a home office deduction. The authors of an article on claiming such deductions (see *The Home Office Lowdown*) state that those who are permitted to claim their home office expenses may also be entitled to claim their transportation expenses to and from the main office. The Treasury Department is not inclined to allow just anybody such a generous double-dip from its coffers. So think twice before claiming the home office deduction.

Getting Zoned In

When I started my remote-control relationship with *Teacher,* I set up shop on the third floor of my house in Philadelphia. But before I moved my desk and computer into my office away from the office, I visited the Department of Licenses and Inspections at city hall to legalize my operation. Elsa, a friend of mine in the neighborhood, took in typing, and she set me wise to the city's home business regulations. In a nutshell, it did not matter whether I was employed by someone else or slaving away for myself. What mattered to the city was the possible disruption to the community should my business prove to be loud, smelly, or toxic or result in customers' cars or delivery trucks blocking the neighbors' driveways.

Of course, I didn't do much smelly or toxic business, and the only visitor I ever had was the Federal Express delivery man and the occasional Jehovah's Witness. Aside from that, no one even knew I was home. I blended into the neighborhood scenery as unobtrusively as Raymond Burr in Hitchcock's *Rear Window*—with the obvious advantage to my neighbors that, unlike Burr's character, I was not a closet homicidal maniac.

I received the city's official imprimatur and never had a problem. I did what I was supposed to do. But many home-based workers never think to look into their local ordinances. Whether they realize it or not, they may be violating local laws. So before you start working at home, you ought to familiarize yourself with the local zoning regs to find out whether you're legal—and what you need to do if you aren't.

The Notion of Zoning

Most modern communities are carved up into zones that limit the kinds of buildings and activities permitted in a particular area. The most common zones are residential, commercial, institutional, and industrial. There can even be zones within zones, depending on such things as the number of houses or apartments the local officials decide can be crammed onto a piece of dirt. A piece of land zoned R-1, for example, might be restricted to single-family houses on an acre of ground. In contrast, a nearby property zoned R-3 might be set aside for a more intensive residential use, such as a townhouse development.

Local zoning restrictions on home-based work were set up to safeguard the community from activities that have the potential to disturb the peace—like backyard welding shops, day-care centers, or, worse yet, day-care centers for welders. However, most zoning laws have long recognized the need for some kind of commercial enterprise in residential areas, so exceptions are made within the regs for certain professions—like doctors' or lawyers' offices. Zoning laws also recognize the need for relatively mild, inoffensive businesses, like typing services, and these are usually permitted. The more intense and obvious the activity—for example, a home-based bake shop employing three or four people, with a fleet of delivery trucks in the driveway—the tighter the restrictions, and the less likely it becomes that they will be permitted within a residential area.

However, all communities are not alike. Some towns, and even some big cities, make no distinction between dinky typing services and larger home-based enterprises, or between the essentially self-employed and the telecommuter, who is employed by someone else and only works at home one day a week. And most municipalities—an estimated nine out of ten, according to the American Planning Association—have at least some restrictions on home employment. That's why it pays to find out whether your intention to work at home is acceptable to the municipal powers that be.

New Zoning Ordinances for Home-Based Workers

As the concept of telecommuting becomes more familiar to local mayors and town councils, zoning laws are being adjusted accordingly. One very good example, frequently cited in zoning and planning literature, is Mount Prospect, Illinois, a community of 53,000 about 22 miles from the Chicago Loop.

Until a few years ago, Mount Prospect zoning law was typically restrictive. It placed severe limits on most home-based workers, with the usual exceptions for doctors and lawyers. Then, in the early '90s, Mount Prospect officials decided to give their zoning laws another look in light of evidence that more and more Americans were taking their work home. "Before, our ordinance was very narrowly constructed, so people who worked from home were technically in violation," says Mount Prospect planner Ken Fritz. "We realized what was going on in the world, and our staff drew up a new ordinance to allow for home-based entrepreneurs and telecommuters. We're being a little bit more realistic about what's happening, and we're allowing those things to take place."

Mount Prospect's ordinance draws no distinction between the self-employed and, say, a manufacturer's rep who occasionally works at home. The law does restrict potentially disruptive influences, like a constant flow of delivery trucks rolling through the neighborhood. If it's a home-based business, the law restricts employees to members of the family, and no signs can be placed in front of the home. None of the work can be done in outbuildings or garages.

How Mount Prospect Governs the Home Worker

Mount Prospect's president and board of trustees passed the village's home-business ordinance in July 1991. Since then it has come to be regarded as a model for the nation. If your town or city doesn't have such an ordinance, or existing laws tend to discriminate against home-based workers, you might want to direct the attention of the town fathers (and mothers, as the case may be) to the Mount Prospect regulation.

Here are the highlights of the Mount Prospect ordinance, courtesy of the Village of Mount Prospect. Note that the law applies equally to telecommuters, who are employed outside the home, and to the owners of home-based businesses.

Purpose: The new ordinance regulates home businesses and home occupations based on the impact of those activities on the surrounding neighborhood.

Definition: A home occupation is defined as "an accessory use conducted completely within a dwelling unit and clearly incidental and secondary to the use of the dwelling for residential purposes. No occupation or part of any occupation shall be conducted in an attached or detached garage. A home occupation may include a for-profit home business or a home office for a resident who may work for another employer or contract or consult with another company or individual."

Standards: Only members of the immediate family residing in the home can be employed in a home occupation. (This is for a home-based business.)

Home occupations shouldn't attract any more visitors than would normally visit a home.

If the home-based business involves private instruction, like music lessons or tutoring, no more than three pupils can visit the house at any one time.

For his part, Fritz believes the community benefits from the new ordinance. If some of those home-based businesses succeed, they may outgrow their cramped quarters and start to fill some of the vacant office buildings in the area. The new ordinance also recognizes the intrinsic value of home-based work to individuals, a lesson that isn't lost on Fritz. "I have a daughter who lives in the community," he says, "and she works for an insurance agency 20 minutes from her home. If things work out, she intends to work at home two or three days a week."

Enabling the Disabled

Gail Colussi laughs when she describes herself as "a walking disaster area." Back in 1982, Gail, an administrator for a federal agency, began to notice some disturbing symptoms. She was seeing double and experiencing numbness on one side of her body. At first she wasn't sure what was wrong, and neither was her doctor. But tests ultimately revealed that Gail was suffering from multiple sclerosis, a chronic disease affecting the nervous system, resulting in a loss of muscle coordination. As if that wasn't bad enough, she has since developed diabetes and chronic hepatitis, which, when it strikes, leaves her exhausted and vulnerable to every little bug.

All of these illnesses have been devastating. Gail, who worked her way up from a file clerk to an administrator, had already been with the agency for more than a dozen years when her MS was diagnosed. Since then, she has frequently been bedridden for anywhere from a week to three months at a time. "Symptoms, mostly poor muscle control and uncoordination, can last anywhere from a week to three months," she explains. "After I had used up all my sick days and vacation time, whenever I was having a real bad attack I wound up borrowing sick time. In our agency we can borrow 40 hours at a time from our future allotment of sick pay with a doctor's documentation. It takes forever to pay it back, and you basically have no sick leave while you're paying it back."

Then, in 1990, Gail's agency initiated the Flexiplace program (also mentioned in Chapter 4), encouraging employees to work at home part time. For Gail, home-based work was the answer to many, many prayers. "Flexiplace began at a good time for me," she says. "At the time, I was having a terrible attack. I couldn't walk without collapsing. I couldn't see. So I started by taking two weeks of sick leave. Then I gradually started working at home, usually one day a week—longer when I needed to, especially if I was having an attack."

Working at home enables Gail to space out her workday, working for two or three hours at a stretch, heading to bed to rest when she needs to, and then going back to work. "While my workday became much longer as a result, I found that I could do my work much more easily. I can also go to my regular Friday doctor's appointment without having to worry about being late getting into the office and having to make up the time."

Most important to Gail, working from her home in northwest Washington gives her a chance to tackle the all-important paperwork upon which government thrives. Like many office workers, she is usually plagued by phone calls and interruptions. Just finding quiet time to think and write while in the main office is often impossible. Before Flexiplace, paper would pile up in her in-box, and as it rose, so did Gail's stress level—which in turn aggravated her illness. In order to complete all her work, she often brought her in-box home with her, working late into the night and over weekends. Now, she says, "Flexiplace has changed all that. I'm much more relaxed. And my weekends are for *me* again."

Home-Based Work Under ADA

Clearly, home-based work has the potential to make life much easier for the disabled—a work option that may be explored further as a result of the federal Americans with Disabilities Act (ADA). Thanks to ADA, some companies may find themselves considering remote employment as a possibility for their disabled workers. In some cases this may be a perfect solution. But in others it may be illegal.

ADA currently requires companies employing 25 or more workers to make reasonable accommodations for their employees who have disabilities. Starting July 26, 1994, the law will also affect companies employing 15 or more. Both employees and employers may find themselves wrestling with the notion of "reasonable accommodation." For instance, an employer may not consider it at all reasonable to provide home-based accommodations for a disabled employee who normally works on an assembly line.

On the other hand, disabled employees in typical office jobs may find home-based work a thoroughly palatable option—particularly those who may not be able to commute long distances due to a mobility impairment. "In many cases, transportation for people like these is lacking or nonexistent," explains Linda Batiste, a human factors consultant for the Job Accommodation Network, an information clearinghouse for workers and employers, based at West Virginia University in Morgantown. "Home-based employment can really be a great option for people who have difficulty getting out of their homes. We get a lot of calls from people who are seeking these kinds of opportunities."

Certainly, recent refinements in communications technology open grand new vistas for the disabled. With voice mail, modems, and fax machines, it often isn't necessary for the worker to even show up at the main office. You could work from your bed if you wanted to—or if you needed to. For disabled workers, this remarkable gadgetry renders the traditional office virtually irrelevant, tearing down the barriers that separate them from fully productive lives. In many cases home-based work seems custom-made for the needs of the disabled. And not just the permanently disabled, either. Some disabilities—like a problem pregnancy—are temporary. As long as home-based work is an option, temporary impairments don't have to cut into an employee's productivity. And as Bonnie High, corporate telecommuting manager at Bell Atlantic, pointed out earlier, offering home-based employment to the permanently or temporarily disabled permits a company to keep highly valued employees.

That said, ADA does not automatically entitle disabled employees to home-based work. Rather, the essence of the law is that it opens the workplace to people who might have been unreasonably kept out of it in the past. The whole idea is to bring disabled workers into the mainstream. "Home-based work *can* be a form of reasonable accommodation," explains Sharon Rennert, ADA technical assistance adviser for the Equal Employment Opportunity Commission. But, she says, "it should not be looked at as the first choice."

More importantly, Rennert says, the law does not permit employers to force disabled employees to work at home against their will—even if they're offering the option "just to be nice." Rennert says, "Employers might assume that just because a person is disabled, he or she might be more comfortable at home. But part of the reason disabled people want to work is that they desire the kind of socialization that goes on at work. They can miss out on all that if they're forced to work at home." Employers might also assume that it's easier and cheaper simply to send a worker home than to install a wheelchair ramp. Or worse, they might be worried that having a disabled employee will make other employees and clients uncomfortable. Under these circumstances, home-based work could be just another name for segregation. And that's illegal.

The bottom line, according to Rennert: If you, as a disabled employee, want to work in the office along with everybody else, ADA requires that the employer find a way to make that possible. If, on the other hand, you want to work at home—or need to, as in the case of Gail Colussi—your employer is obligated to hear you out. But under no circumstances should a disabled employee be required to work at home as a condition of employment, just because the employer assumes it's easier all around. As Rennert says, "'Easier all around' can translate into discrimination."

CHAPTER 6

AVOIDING PROFESSIONAL PITFALLS

Wendell Joice, like most work-at-homers, was grateful to be on his own. At times he couldn't believe he had stumbled onto such a good thing. While others were sitting in a big federal office building, assaulted by the jangle of ringing telephones, the robotic stuttering of fax machines, and ceaseless human prattle, Wendell, a personnel research psychologist and personnel manager for the Office of Personnel Management, was at peace in his cozy home office. He was so happy, in fact, and so utterly lacking in distractions, that he was completely consumed by his work. At 4:30 P.M., when his colleagues were making their way home, catching the Metro out to Silver Spring or tooling down I-66 to Manassas, Wendell was still plugging away at the computer. And well after the dinner hour, when his co-workers were kicking back, sipping a well-deserved aperitif, and tuning in to *Roseanne,* Wendell was poring over reports, planning the next day's meetings, and responding to his mail.

See Wendell work. See Wendell overachieve. See Wendell's head explode like a watermelon.

For Wendell Joice, as for many of those who respond to the often irresistible siren song of the home office, having the flexibility to work whenever you want, as long as you want, was both a blessing and curse. "I got real wrapped up in my work," he says. "A little *too* wrapped up. In the beginning, as I first started taking work home with me, I discovered that I could spend all my time in my office. Soon I realized that I was exhausted all the time. I was no longer having any fun. I wasn't socializing, going out with my friends. I'd look up at the clock and realize that I'd kept right on working late into the evening. So I asked myself: If working at home is really so much more efficient, how come I'm working harder than ever before?"

Home-based work *is* a good thing. But sometimes it can be too *much* of a good thing. For those who are more conventionally employed, the office is a place you can leave behind at the end of the day. But when you have an office in your home, in some sense you are always at work. A thought occurs. The computer beckons. No matter that it is 4:30 in the morning.

For some telecommuters, of course, laboring too hard isn't the problem. Getting organized and getting started are the more pressing concerns. Becoming motivated to work at home can also be a powerful concern. If the circumstances of your home-based job leave you feeling lonely—perhaps you're home too much—you may find that the charm wears off quickly. I'll deal with that in Chapter 8.

But for those of us who were workaholics to begin with, having a fully equipped office in the home is like being a sugar addict and working in a candy factory. Overwork is a real hazard, one of many professional perils and pitfalls associated with home-based employment.

In this chapter I'll explore many of the dangers, tolls, and snares of working at home and how to deal with them. I'll also consider the often expressed worry about isolation. What's happening at the office when you aren't there? Could what you don't know hurt you? And finally, I'll look at the possible impact of home-based work on your career. Will your employer view your decision to work at home as a sign that you aren't really committed?

I'll begin with the often all-consuming issue of overwork.

KNOW WHEN TO SAY WHEN

When we say all-consuming, we mean it. Too much work can eat you alive. It can take an otherwise nice guy and turn him into a tired, listless, grouchy SOB who snaps at his wife and snarls at his cat.

But enough about me. Let's consider the case of Duncan Dieterly, who, as an industrial psychologist, ought to know a thing or two about how the mind works—literally and figuratively. One of the driving forces behind Southern California Edison's telecommuting program, Dieterly is an enthusiastic proponent of home-based work. Yet even he found that he was not immune to excess toil in the corporate vineyards. When you work at home even part of the time, he notes, "your first problem is that the office is so accessible. You find that you have unbelievable amounts of time to get work done. I remember the first day I brought work home with me. I had everything done in half a day. I had an early tendency to work too much. I never took any breaks. By about two o'clock in the afternoon, I would be very tired."

Travelers systems information specialist Janet Reincke had the same problem. "I've always had so much to do that I could just get up out of bed and start working," she says. "I really could work 24 hours a day and never get it all done."

Why do they do it? What makes an otherwise sane individual take on a completely irrational workload? Well, many do it simply because they *can*. Having an office in your home means never having to clock out. This was Dieterly's experience. But he and others have learned that the following techniques help them cope:

- **Keep a regular schedule.** This doesn't mean you have to work from nine to five—what's the point? But if you were working in a conventional office setting, you would start working at a particular time and end work eight or nine hours later. Just because you can work 12 hours a day doesn't mean you have to.

- **Take frequent breaks.** If you were in the office, you might wander down to the cafeteria at about 10 A.M. for a cup of coffee. At 3 P.M. you might take a walk around the office park. You probably wouldn't enter your office at 7 A.M., close the door, and not re-emerge until sundown. "I literally had to make myself take a break every two or three hours," says Dieterly. "The other thing I did was to make a short list of people I needed to call so it would break up my workday."
- **Close the office door.** You should develop a routine for ending your workday, a way of saying, in so many words, "it's Miller time." Turn off the computer. Forward all your calls to voice mail. Switch off the light, shut the door behind you, and don't re-enter the office until tomorrow. This is easier said than done. When you know that the office is not an hour and a half but rather a few steps away, the temptation is often great to sit down at your desk in the wee hours and hammer out the details of your big sales pitch. But you should tell yourself that the office is closed.

It's also a good idea to locate your office as far off the beaten track as possible. If you can avoid it, don't set up your desk and computer in your bedroom or anywhere near it. Create a gap between your work and the rest of your life. Put some distance between yourself and your in-basket, or you will quickly find that it is always full. You will always think of things to do.

Sometimes, even if you want to keep work at arm's length, you may feel obligated to put in long hours simply because others expect you to do so. After all, you've been given a privilege. You want to work hard to be worthy of your supervisor's trust. In a sense, the legendary hyperproductivity of telecommuters works against them. Supervisors begin to ask for too much, thinking that there's nothing a well-organized home-based worker can't do. And like Ado Annie in

Oklahoma!, employees who are new to the remote workplace find that they "cain't say no."

Here's how Jane Menaker, a Fort Lauderdale insurance claims representative, describes the process: "When I first started working at home, I went through a variety of stages. In the first stage, people ask you to do more and more, and you don't feel comfortable declining. Then, in the next stage, you start to get resentful. Finally, you reach the stage where you begin to decline, sometimes not very politely. But that's what you have to do."

Know Your Limits

To keep from becoming overwhelmed by work, home-based employees must learn to develop a set of skills—the first one being how and when to say no. Setting priorities is part of your job. If you tackled every single project and acceded to every unreasonable demand in the conventional office setting, everyone would wonder about your sanity. If you think about it, negotiating with other people to get them to do things, and vice versa, is what work is all about. Changing the circumstances of your employment requires an adjustment on the part of your colleagues, supervisors, and clients. Just because you have reverted to working at home one or two days a week doesn't mean you have unlimited time, energy, and freedom. You have to let others know that. If you don't tell them that you aren't Superman, they'll keep on asking you to leap tall buildings in a single bound. As Jane Menaker puts it, "I've come to understand that it is my responsibility to help those people around me make the transition to my new schedule. I can't expect others to understand without my telling them the day-to-day details of my schedule."

Finally, some telecommuters are overburdened and stressed out because they expect more of themselves in virtually every respect. They make the mistake of believing that, because they are home, they can take on even more domestic responsibilities than before. That's so easy to do if you're home. Home is where the laundry is.

Home is where the dirty kitchen floor is. Just because you're home, you come to believe—and perhaps your spouse blithely assumes—that you should be able to do it all.

This is a particular problem for women. No doubt about it, you *can* do more, and that's one of the wonderful benefits of home-based work. But it's a huge mistake for you, or your spouse, to think that you can do two jobs all by yourself.

Jane Menaker found that she needed to set her husband straight in the same way she dealt with her colleagues at work. "I've learned to be very clear about what I have time to do at home," she explains. "At the beginning, my husband would assume that because I was home, I would make dinner. He'd come home and wonder why dinner wasn't on the table. Sometimes I would have the time, but frequently I didn't. And so he and I had to sit down and divide the household labor, right down to the tiniest detail. I'd say, 'I have an interview by phone starting at five o'clock. If we're going to eat at six, you're going to have to make dinner."

Fight Separation Anxiety

One day not too long ago, I walked into my boss's office, wanting to know why I hadn't seen much of my co-worker Joe lately. "Is he on vacation?" I asked. Pat responded, a look of incredulity crossing her face, "You must be joking."

Joe was on a very long vacation indeed. The longest, in fact. He had quit about a week before and was working somewhere else. Now, things like this don't happen to me all the time, and to be fair, Joe wasn't even in my department. It wasn't like I saw him every day. But my experience does show that you can miss out on a good deal of useful information on those days when you aren't in the office.

Not all the office news finds its way into the company newsletter. Typically, everything *important* I know about work I learn from the company gossips: who's a rising star, who's on the way out, whether we had a good response to our direct-mail campaign, whether we got the grant. Reading between the lines, you can usually get a good sense of what might happen next at your company and how whatever happens could affect you.

Charlie Wolfson worked as a technology ad sales representative for a small, entrepreneurial newsletter publishing company in Lanham, Maryland. Because he lived about two hours away, in Wilmington, Delaware, his supervisor agreed to let him telecommute practically every day. His only window on the soul of the firm was a monthly staff meeting, which he attended without fail. "In none of the meetings I attended did I detect a sense of impending doom. And because I was rarely in the main office, I never picked up on the telltale signs that something was wrong," he says.

Unbeknownst to Wolfson, his firm was in big trouble. Though the owner was playing things pretty close to the vest, other employees started to notice early warning signs. The once gregarious, affable owner suddenly became withdrawn and sullen. Stern-looking visitors arrived for all-day closed-door meetings. Plans for a big, costly project were abruptly cancelled. The office manager suddenly had strict orders to scrimp on everything, from business travel to paper clips.

Then one day the layoffs came. While his in-office colleagues had become suspicious, Charlie never saw trouble coming. "If I'd been in the office every day, I might at least have had an inkling," he says. "Other people apparently did, but they were all so wrapped up in their own worries that no one thought to tell me. The first time I knew something was wrong was the day I received my notice of separation."

From the very start of her telecommuting adventure, Cheri Shore, manufacturing rep and systems design consultant for Pacific Bell, has made it a point never to get caught short in the same way Charlie Wolfson was. Cheri is a true believer in the importance of scuttlebutt. "In any large corporation, the office rumor mill is a very important information source," she says. "When you don't work in the main office, you tend to get left out of things." Cheri countered this problem by developing other information sources, such as regular telephone calls to her old friends.

Again, based on the experience of Cheri and others, it's a very good idea to cultivate this personal type of insider information. Make it a point to have regular in-person or telephone chats with your supervisor or your old colleagues and spies. Don't wait for meetings to visit your old stomping ground. If you're lucky enough to have a full-time telecommuting agreement, don't go native.

It is oh so easy for full-time telecommuters to develop a kind of lone wolf mentality, like the Marlon Brando character who went up the river and over the edge in *Apocalypse Now.* Without too much difficulty, you can isolate yourself from the rest of the world. Be on guard against this insular outlook. Leave your little island paradise for frequent, semi-unplanned visits to civilization. Don't wait for an engraved invitation to a staff meeting.

The Eight Best Ways to Keep in Touch

Want to make sure they don't sell the company while you aren't looking? Or do you just want to make sure your colleagues, yon Mr. Cassius and Mr. Brutus, aren't secretly plotting your downfall? Here's how to make your presence felt in the office.

1. Keep your home days to a minimum. Suppose you have the freedom to work at home as often as you like. Not probable, but stranger things have happened. Don't do it. If you want to guarantee that you'll be forgotten, staying home every day is the best way to do it. Two days a week at home is usually about right. Three days may be stretching it.

2. Don't stay home during crunch times. If an important project deadline is fast approaching, don't adhere rigidly to your home-based schedule. Even if you can do the work just as easily at home,

in the eyes of your colleagues—and perhaps your supervisor—you aren't there when you're needed most.

3. Cultivate spies. Every office has a gossip—or two or three. Often, with their keen powers of observation, they know what's going on before anyone else has caught on. *You* know who these people are. Make sure you chat with one of them on the days you're home, and make arrangements to have coffee with them when you return to the office.

4. Ask a co-worker or secretary to check your in-box on the days you're at home. It might be one of the unwritten laws of nature that important mail or memos arrive when you aren't there to receive them. If you don't have E-mail, it's especially important to have someone keep an eye on incoming letters. Check in once a day to see if there is any important news.

5. Offer your home as a meeting place. Clearly, the folks in your division aren't always going to be able to pack everything up and head out into the suburbs. But in most jobs, meetings are occasionally called for the purpose of planning and brainstorming. These meetings are often more productive outside the office, where people don't have to worry as much about distractions. So if the occasion warrants, invite your supervisor and co-workers to join you on your deck for a day in the sun. And take the opportunity to show them your home office setup. Let them see that you're really working.

6. Use your E-mail. If you have the capability, make certain you keep in touch electronically. Let the folks at the office know that Big Brother—or Big Sister—is watching.

7. Don't forget to socialize. If you and your colleagues usually head out to the neighborhood taproom on Thursday nights for some much-needed rest and relaxation, try to make time to join them. If the usual watering hole is inconvenient, suggest that the group try a new place halfway between your home and the main office.

8. Remember the little things. When you're in the main office, you're often approached for donations for birthday presents, shower gifts, and the like. If you're male, and like most of the men I know—myself included—you probably don't keep a list of birthdays and

special occasions in your calendar. Before you embark on your work-at-home adventure, be sure to make such a list. Send cards at the appropriate times and remember to chip in money for gifts. If you aren't physically present, probably no one will think to ask you if you want to participate. And nothing makes a home-based worker feel more left out than to hear of parties and special events held in his or her absence.

Protect Your Interests

Are you a team player? Maybe *you* think so, but in the eyes of some managers, if you work at home you might as well be a third-string has-been with bum knees. Nolan Ryan you ain't. The company may see you as less than a fully functional, wholly committed member of the team.

This may not be the case in all firms. At Aetna, for example, the company's recent survey of telecommuters and their bosses revealed that more than 90 percent of home-based workers received merit increases, according to company spokesman Denise Cichon. Fully 70 percent received bonuses for their performance.

At Bell Atlantic, 3 of 50 employees in the company's pilot program were promoted, a fairly representative proportion, according to Bonnie High, manager of corporate telecommuting. "Your career here doesn't become derailed if you telecommute," she says.

But for Rollins College professor Donald Rogers, a longtime observer of telecommuting, the central issues of reward and advancement are very real concerns for some employees. "'How will this affect my career?' That's the one question people ask," he says. "A lot of people simply aren't going to be willing to telecommute because they are afraid it will damage their career. In fast-track organizations, like commercial real estate firms and the big financial houses, the feeling is that you've got to be there every day."

You may be able to nip career concerns in the bud by asking your employer to enumerate some clear procedures for reward and promotion as part of your formal written telecommuting agreement, says telecommuting expert Kathleen Christensen. This was less of a concern for the first generation of telecommuters, she says, because many of the earliest home-based workers were computer techies, more interested in the technology than in advancement. Or they were star performers who didn't have to worry about rising to the top. It may not be as easy with succeeding generations, which will include many less obviously sterling employees. The whole issue of promotion and career advancement may pose a problem for them, she says, unless the firm is truly committed to widespread cultural change and is willing to reward telecommuting job performance.

In the absence of a mutually agreed upon set of standards by which your performance is measured, you may be taking a chance with your career. Deciding whether the benefits outweigh the risks is up to you. In Donald Rogers's review of telecommuting literature, he finds that women in particular complain that working at home has knocked a few rungs out of their climb up the corporate ladder. "It causes a break in their careers from which some say they never completely recover, or one that fundamentally changes their career in some negative way."

But this is far from universally true. In a piece entitled "Being Smart About the Mommy Track" in *Working Woman* (February 1993), authors Barbara Kantrowitz and Pat Wingert point out that because of changing corporate attitudes, many women are finding that flexible schedules no longer brand them as less serious about their work than their nine-to-five peers. "Companies are realizing that in order to attract and keep skilled female staffers—the majority of whom are in their childbearing years—they have to respond to their needs as both employees and mothers," the authors write. In fact, some mothers who cut back on their in-office time actually manage to *advance* their career while working a reduced schedule. But such women, of course, are still the exception, not the rule.

Sometimes, even if your company continues to look favorably on your performance, accepting your just reward—promotion—may mean giving up your home-based work routine. By saying no, you could hold up your own progress within the firm. Crestar benefits compensation executive Donelle Glatz has been offered two opportunities for promotion since she began working at home. Both times she has turned down these opportunities for advancement, since the new positions would mean returning to the standard nine-to-five schedule. "After a while, I believe they're going to stop asking," she concedes. "That's OK. I don't feel a bit negative about it. I'm getting the opportunity to see my kids grow up, to prepare good meals, and to kiss my husband. I feel good about my family life. Some day my kids will be grown and gone, and I can always go back to doing something else if I need to feel like a big cheese."

Donelle notes that this is her second marriage. In her first marriage, she says, both she and her husband were far too focused on succeeding at their jobs, which "doesn't get you anywhere at home."

According to Donald Rogers, this attitude epitomizes the beliefs of many young executives today. Unlike some of their older coworkers, they put family first. Maybe they're risking their careers. But on the other hand, they're gaining time to be with their children and spouses, which often means far more to them. Whether the career impediments posed by home-based work represent a peril to you depends largely on your personal priorities.

"Typically, people who ask whether working at home is going to hurt them are gung-ho careerists," Rogers says. "But the people who realize that telecommuting could slow their rise to the top of the corporate ladder and want to do it anyway are people who really don't want or ever expect to be president or vice president of the company. What they expect to be is a department manager, a team leader—a middle- to upper-level management position. They're usually more realistic than the gung-ho careerist. Their personal and family life is more important to them."

Tales From the Front: How Telecommuters Cope

Work at home often enough and you'll soon learn new coping skills. You'll learn how to stay sane when the walls are closing in. You'll figure out the best ways to stay in touch. All telecommuters have stories to tell about how they adjusted to their new work style. Here's a completely unscientific, thoroughly random sampling of home-based-worker views.

"I regularly work with a partner on most major writing projects," says Ann Sheihing, who co-edits her company's newsletter. "When I'm in the office, she and I are practically inseparable. So when I work at home, we maintain regular communication. We don't let a day go by without keeping in touch by phone at least once or twice. She's my main source of information about what's going on at work in my absence. Talking to her also keeps me from going stark raving mad in my home office. The other benefit when you call in as often as I do is that no one forgets you."

Sally Hughes, an accountant, is highly motivated, a proven self-starter. Still, there are times when even she feels the pressure of work intruding on her home life. To keep home feeling like home, she likes to remind herself of the pleasures of home-based work. "Every once in a while during the day, I do something domestic," she says. "I prepare lunch. I make a phone call to one of my friends and just chat about our families, plans for the weekend, things like that. Other times I like to do laundry. I'm usually well organized enough so that if I feel like breaking up the day by going shopping or running errands, then that's what I'll do. I don't have to sit at my desk from nine to five like I would in a 'real' office."

Newspaper columnist Barbra Hepler's central concern is communication. "I'm really determined to make this arrangement work," she says. "I wouldn't want to lose my days at home because I was perceived as being out of touch. So I've developed several routines that I follow religiously. When someone from the office calls me at home, I call back ASAP. I don't wait even a couple of hours. I call my voice mail at night so I know what's waiting for me when I go into the office the next day. And I make it a point to change my voice mail messages, both at home and at the office, daily. It's always so annoying to get someone's voice mail with an old recording that they haven't changed for a week. If they haven't bothered to update their phone greeting, you have to wonder whether they've even checked their messages. It creates a very bad impression."

For Harry Humes, a poet and professor in the English department at Kutztown University in south-central Pennsylvania, keeping work in its place is never a concern. "About five or six years ago, we fixed up an old shed out in back of the house," he says. "When I need to work, I can walk out the back door of my house, cross a stream, and climb up a ladder to my room among the maples. It's a lot more pleasant up there, and the view's nicer. I have a lot more of *my* things that I'm surrounded by...like my picture of Babe Ruth."

Medical textbook editor Veronica Newland works at home on Tuesdays and Thursdays. Her success hinges on careful planning. "When I started taking work home two years ago, I had to organize my days carefully, to decide what I could do at home and what I should be doing at the office," she says. "As I went along, gaining experience, that kind of preparation came naturally. I copy all of my work onto disks that I carry back and forth, so I never get home and discover that I left a chapter at the office. I also try to maintain a record in my notebook of where I keep important items in the main office, like contracts or letters from authors, so I can tell the secretary where they are if I call in. I always check my home office carefully before leaving for work the next day to make sure I haven't accidentally left something behind."

CHAPTER 7

SETTING UP SHOP

Ideally, the home-based worker should be snugly ensconced in a quiet, cheery, and, if possible, *private* office, with all the necessary supplies within reach, and never more than a quick phone call away from the main office. The home office should be your sanctuary away from the clamor of the center-city office tower, yes—trying to find a little peace is one of the reasons many of us work at home—but it should not be so calming as to induce slumber.

You don't need to have custom-made barrister shelving, a leather CEO chair, and an antique oak desk. On the other hand, your accommodations should not be needlessly Spartan. After all, you have to *work* here. You might as well try to be comfortable. You may not need a computer, but if you do need one it might not have to be the latest, most expensive model, with all the costliest designer software—especially if all you do is write. You should, of course, be easily accessible by telephone. Though a fax could be useful, it might not be a necessity.

Up to now, this book has been concerned primarily with an exploration of work-at-home strategies—whether telecommuting is for you, how to plan your move, how to talk the supervisor into letting you go, and what your life might be like once you make the switch. Now I'm going to address some of the all-important nuts and bolts. That is, once you've committed to working at home, how should you set up your office? Where should it be? What should it contain?

Clearly, I can't cover every possible contingency, but I can give you some broadly useful ideas for how to operate in your office-away-from-the-office.

Space: The Final Frontier

There are some people who could work quite efficiently propped up on orange crates smack in the middle of I-95. Minnesota data-entry clerk Cathy Kuehl, with her desk set up in the basement alongside the pool table, strikes me as that type of person. But for most of us, there is a distinct relationship between where we work and *how* we work.

Take, for instance, what happens if you work at the dining room table. If your family's dining room table is like mine, it often functions as a combination in-box/mail room/toy-sorting area. *Not* the best place in the house to leave your files from work. If you do work there, you probably have to move everything before dinner, especially if you don't want your files to be mistaken for junk mail and tossed into the trash. Very inconvenient. And when you move your stuff, where do you put it? On the coffee table? Into your briefcase? On the bed, until after the dinner dishes are cleared?

Lisa Kanorek is a professional consultant who makes it her business to help home-based workers get sorted out. One of the first things she recommends is that you set up a work area in a quiet place that is separate from the rest of the house and away from such distractions as the refrigerator and the television. This could be in a spare bedroom or, like Cathy Kuehl's "office," in the basement. Or it could even be a large closet that has been gutted and converted into a sort of work cubby.

"Physically, your work space has to be separate from everything else," says Kanorek, author of *Organizing Your Home Office for Success* (New American Library/Plume). "You have to know that when you enter that space, you are there to work. You don't use it for pleasure."

That said, home offices don't have to be cells. Your desk can be an attractive and useful piece of furniture. It doesn't have to be war-surplus gray metal. You can fill your bookshelves with important reference books and work manuals *and* that large picture of you and your spouse dressed up like Bonnie and Clyde, taken at the Jersey shore.

And by all means, give considerable thought to lighting. If you're working on a computer all day long, you may want soft, indirect light to minimize glare. Or if you can't escape bright light, purchase a glare screen for your computer. (You could also try moving your computer.) And don't feel obliged to face the wall, says Kanorek. Pivoting your desk so it faces the office door or a window can sometimes give you a different and refreshing perspective.

Beyond that, says Kanorek, a successful home office generally has these characteristics:

- **Vertical design.** Even if your office at work is fairly spacious, in all likelihood your office space at home will be rather small. You don't have lots of room to spread *out,* so you're going to have to build *up*. One example of this concept is the rolling computer cart that takes up very little horizontal space but provides plenty of vertical space for your computer, monitor, printer, and printer paper. Another example, of course, is shelving. Get everything off the floor and onto the wall.
- **A "work circle."** "Sit at your desk and spread your arms out in front of you and alongside you," says Kanorek. "Everything should be within arm's reach. If you have to leave the office to get a fax, for example, you are looking for trouble. Outside the office there are too many distractions."
- **Ample storage space.** If you have a spare closet, fill it with everything you're going to need to do your work.
- **A well-located computer.** If you use a computer in your work, it is very likely the center of all your activity. Make sure you put your desk in a place where you aren't likely to

trip over the printer cable every time you get up to go to the bathroom.

- **A good chair.** You could be one of those people who is quite at home sitting on a folding metal chair. But most of us, after an hour or so of sitting in one of those chairs, find that our buns feel like they're made of metal, too, and our spines are beginning to fold. Folding metal chairs weren't made for long-term desk work. Yet as important as a comfortable chair is, Kanorek says, "that's where most people skimp."

  Shop around for a chair that adequately supports your back, one that is adjustable so you can raise and lower the backrest and elevate and lower the seat. If you still aren't comfortable, purchase a back cushion. Armrests are very useful when you must type for long periods.

  By the way, while you're seated, keep both feet on the floor. If your feet don't reach, shorty, buy or make a nonskid footrest you can plant your tootsies on. A clear plastic mat is also nice to have as you roll your chair back and forth. It keeps your wheels from hanging up in carpeting, keeps rugs from getting worn, and reduces the static electricity.

- **Minimal clutter.** This is your office, not Pier 1 Imports. "Resist the idea that your office should be a dumping ground," says Kanorek. Keep stuff off the floor. Put the exercise bike somewhere else. Move the sewing machine. Put supplies in a closet or on shelves installed for that purpose. And remember that supplies come in big boxes that can only add to the clutter. Break out only the number of paper clips or pencils or sheets of printer paper you think you're going to need, and keep them in neat plastic bins. Store the rest in the basement or the garage.

  You might want to have a small radio or shelf-style stereo cassette player if you work better with music. But one entertainment appliance should never show its big eye in your office—the television.

By the way, you might find that planning your home office gives

THE HOME OFFICE ENVIRONMENTAL CHECKLIST

Set up your office in a room separate from the bedroom, living room, and kitchen—as far off the beaten path as possible. You *could* work at the kitchen table, *if* you lived alone in a small efficiency apartment, *if* you didn't have to worry about children using your spreadsheets for Ninja Turtle masks, and *if* you possessed such incredible self-control that you were able to resist the siren song of Heath Bar Crunch frozen yogurt calling to you from your freezer.

If at all possible, make sure your office has a door that you can close to seal out interruptions and to further reinforce the idea that while you are in this room, you are on the clock. (See *Lead Yourself Not Into Temptation* in Chapter 8.)

Try to keep all of your important equipment—the phone, the computer, the printer, the fax machine—within easy reach. Having to get off the phone to retrieve a fax or examine a printout is a waste of motion.

Take all the summer clothes, the model trains, or whatever other stowaways you have in your office closet and find another place for them. You should have a handy place to store supplies in or conveniently near your office. If you don't have a closet, set up a shelf system in your office. Try to keep the shelves stocked with all the necessities. Interrupting your workday to run down to the stationery store for a ream of printer paper is not the best use of your time.

Choose a desk and chair carefully, particularly if you'll be using a computer for long periods.

Again, if you expect to be doing close-up work, like word processing—a task previously and primitively known as writing—you should have bright, indirect lighting. Aunt Harriet's hand-me-down gooseneck lamp won't cut it.

you a fresh new perspective on your office at work. After all, says Kanorek, "Getting organized is not something most of us are taught."

Some other useful tips:

"The first thing I usually recommend to prospective telecommuters," says consultant Joanne Pratt, "is that people draw a picture of their home and pinpoint on that picture where the office is going to be. Then do an enlarged diagram of the office space and try to be realistic about where the computer is going to be, where the phone lines and the electrical outlets are, what kind of light is coming in, whether there's a safe place for confidential materials, and so on. I try to get them to imagine ahead of time what this work space is going to be like."

"Once you've set up your home office, take a picture of it and show it to your supervisor," says Pratt. "It might reassure the supervisor that you have an appropriate space in which to do your work."

Almost Like Being There

Whether you work at home one day a week or every day, one tool is essential: the telephone. Undoubtedly you have one, but a lot has been happening to the phone recently.

The answering machine was perhaps the most exotic telecommunications device up until a few years ago. No question about it, the answering machine is as essential to the home-based worker as are microwave popcorn and coffee. Local phone companies now offer a range of services that can make your existing telephone much more useful. Some can make your answering machine look pretty shabby by comparison.

Recently, the local Baby Bell that serves my area sent me a listing of all the new services available to the residential customer: call waiting, call forwarding, three-way calling, speed calling, repeat call, return call, caller ID, home intercom, and voice mail. There's even a service marketed locally as Identa Ring that allows a customer to operate more than one telephone number off one line. Each line is assigned a distinct number of rings, letting you know whether you're receiving a business call or a personal call.

(Before we go on, let me say that this is definitely *not* an unpaid ad for the telecommunications industry of America. Personally, I couldn't care less who you reach out and touch, or even how. That said...)

Let's consider what happens when your boss tries to call you but you are on the phone with a colleague or client. Maybe your boss is the trusting type, and she assumes you're talking business. But maybe she is the imaginative type who assumes that, at best, you have the phone off the hook while you take a nap, or, at worst, you're ordering box-seat tickets to next week's doubleheader.

The point is simply this: If you are working at home, the best way to ensure that you continue to enjoy this privilege is to make sure the arrangement is easy on your boss, your colleagues, and your customers. If everyone has to jump through hoops to find and work with you, then this relationship may not last. Ideally, no one who calls you should be able to tell that you aren't in the main office. Your work-at-home lifestyle should be transparent. Telephone services like voice mail make this possible.

When Joe Hearn isn't at his desk at the GTE main office in Irving, Texas, callers to his office number usually hear a voice mail announcement asking them to leave a message. What they may not know is that his office telephone is rigged up to activate his personal electronic pager whenever he receives a message, wherever he happens to be. The beeper displays his office telephone number, which clues him in to the fact that a message is waiting. He checks his voice mail and returns the call. No one who calls his office number has any idea that he is anywhere *but* in his office.

As new-product manager for GTE in Texas, Hearn is responsible for developing products and services for the work-at-home market in about 30 states. Hearn says new services offered by his company and others can make telecommuters far more productive—even though they might increase the monthly telephone bill.

GTE, like many telecommunications companies, is putting its

services to the ultimate test, using its own employees in a pilot telecommuting program. Among the services offered to employees, for example, is access to company computers via modem. Hearn says, "The possibility of getting into their electronic mail from home covers a very large percentage of the communications requirements that they would have if they were in the office. My employees refer to their time at home as 'clean time.' They don't have as many interruptions. They have voice mail service and can call in and check their messages whenever they want to."

Hearn himself takes advantage of the opportunity to work at home about one day a week. For him, working at home means being able to avoid travel on the LBJ Highway, the busiest route in Texas. "Being able to avoid that, even once a week, makes me feel much better about my workday," he says.

John Bellarini, who works for Bell Atlantic in the mid-Atlantic states, performs a function similar to Hearn's, helping to popularize telecommuting. In Bellarini's case, however, the job is not developing new products but helping corporations set up their own telecommuting programs. And the one thing all telecommuters want, he says, is the ability to communicate by telephone in a way that does not draw attention to their off-site work arrangement. "People who telecommute believe that their arrangement is a perk, and they want to make it worthwhile to the company by being in contact all the time," he says. "They want to respond immediately."

Hold the Phone

There are so many new services available to home-based workers who want to stay in touch that you may not be familiar with them all. Talk with your phone company's customer service representative to determine what products are offered. In the meantime, here are some of the more popular options:

- **Voice mail.** Marketed under such names as "Personal Secretary" and "Answer Call," voice mail is really an improvement on your home answering machine. Your answering machine can take messages when you aren't home, but can it intercept messages when you are on the telephone? If you have one of the many forms of voice mail offered by telephone companies, you have this flexibility, as well as the option to save or delete messages. If you want to know the time and date when a message was left, you can find out by pressing a couple of buttons.

Voice mail also allows you to set up mailboxes to separate calls for you from calls for your wife or teenage son. You can transfer messages from one mailbox to another. And you can even send reminders to yourself, recording a message and timing the call to arrive at a given time, to remind you of appointments or errands. As with most commercial answering machines, you can check your message from pretty much anywhere.

- **Call waiting.** While you are on the phone, a tone alerts you if someone else wants to talk to you. Nice to have most of the time, but a genuine pain when the person who interrupts your very important call is selling aluminum siding or wants you to buy encyclopedias.
- **Ring identifier.** If you're home alone and you really need to screen out all but essential business communication, you may want a service such as Indent-a-ring that enables you to tell simply by the number of rings whether the incoming call is a business or a personal call.

  This service enables you to have more than one telephone number, but on one line. You might use a service like this if you want to maintain one number as a fax line, but you wouldn't be able to use the phone while a fax was being received. (If you think you're going to need a fax machine, and you expect to use it a lot, consider a separate second line.)
- **Fax switcher.** Suppose a fax comes for you on the main office fax machine. Using this service you can divert the fax to your home-office fax.

- **Call forwarding.** Many phone companies offer this very useful option. Bell Atlantic, for example, calls the service Ultra Forward. On those days when you work at home, you can set up your office telephone to automatically transfer all calls to your home phone line.
- **Three-way calling.** Do you really need it? "People can answer this question by asking how many times a week they conference call with colleagues at work," says Sandy Grantow, consumer service representative for Bell Atlantic. "With this service you could hook up your client and your boss, or your lawyer and your accountant."

Summary of Phone Services

Voice mail. Takes and saves messages; intercepts messages while you're on the phone.

Call waiting. Alerts you when you're on the phone that someone else is trying to reach you.

Ring identifier. Lets you know whether a call is business or personal.

Fax switcher. Diverts faxes from your main office to your home fax.

Call forwarding. Transfers calls from your office phone to your home phone.

Three-way calling. Lets you make conference calls.

Computers and Other Gizmos

Do you need a computer? What kind? Will a desktop model do, or do you think you need a laptop? What kind of software? How do you install it?

When you reported for work on the first day, there may have

been a computer already set up on your desk, loaded with software and ready to run. But if you don't have a computer at home, and you think you're going to need one, all sorts of questions pop into your head.

When I purchased my computer a few years ago, I had a substantial advantage: Mike Aubin, resident systems operator at *Teacher*, who advised me on my equipment purchase and loaded all the software and installed all the hardware he thought I was going to need to transmit stories from my home in Philly to the magazine's mainframe computer in Washington. I was so thankful for his help that I bought him some gift certificates for the Hard Rock Cafe, but when I look back now on how useful his contribution has turned out to be, my thanks doesn't seem like enough. A competent systems operator is worth his weight in chips.

Without Mike's help, I'm not really certain what I would have done. And now things are even more complicated. When I bought my Epson 286, IBM-compatible, high-powered applications like Windows were just coming into vogue. I *could* run Windows on my 286, but road kill has been known to move faster. Fortunately, all I need is a word processor. I don't do spreadsheets. I don't do computer-aided design. I don't do Windows. Now, however, computers with 386 and 486 microprocessors—capable of running very high-powered applications—are available for less than what I paid just a few years ago for my then state-of-the-art 286. What's more, there's a veritable universe of sexy applications available that run on the faster, more powerful machines.

Buying one of these monsters is one thing. Learning to run it is quite another. What do you do with your supercharged, water-cooled, hemi-under-glass, rocket-assisted 486 once you have it out of the box? And should you be buying one of these IBM-compatibles, or looking into one of the new Apples? It is a puzzlement.

Help From a Computer Nerd

Enter Mike Wyckoff, who until a few years ago fixed computers for a large company in Virginia. On the side he helped friends and acquaintances set up their home computers, loading software, offering advice on equipment purchases, and making house calls when screens froze up or files disappeared into the ether. After a while he realized that home-computer owners needed a kind of on-call systems operator, and so he started his own company: Rent-A-Nerd, based in Vienna, Virginia, soon to become a national franchise. Rent-A-Nerd's services are available to the everyday working stiff at a rate of a buck a minute.

"Right now, there isn't anybody going after our market niche," explains Wyckoff, whose business card reads: Head Nerd. "The problem is, systems consultants and consulting firms aren't interested in small fry. They seek out the large corporate contracts. We do just the opposite. The majority of our business is under two hours a call. Our market is individuals and small businesses. Our billing structure is set up in such a way as to make it as painless as possible. We're kind of like the Kmart of computer consultants."

In Wyckoff's experience, most new computer owners have similar problems. They want to know which computer to buy, what kind of peripherals to use—printers, modems, mice (or mouses?), drives—how to load software, and whether the software will run on a particular model.

Wyckoff's tips for beginners:

What kind of computer should I buy?

Roughly 90 percent of all U.S. businesses run on IBMs or compatibles, according to Wyckoff. If your company is among them, you'll probably want to buy a compatible computer. But keep your eye on Apple.

Apples have been less popular in the business market because of their proprietary operating system, Wycoff says. IBM-type computers are based on the Disk Operating System (DOS), a kind of lingua franca, or common language, that enables you to type up a report on your Epson at home and run it on your Compudyne at work. Until recently, Apple's system wasn't compatible with DOS. But now "System 7" Apples are available that will run DOS programs, giving the user more choice. Apple, of course, set the industry standard for ease of use. DOS was outright klutzy compared to Apple's pioneering system of graphic cues, or icons. Windows applications, of course, are now available for use on IBM-compatibles, and they offer similar ease of use. So whether you choose IBM or Apple is no longer the biggest concern. It's really which operating environment you prefer.

Visit the computer store and take a number of models for a test drive before you make a purchase. And if you buy an Apple, make sure it's one that will run DOS programs if all your office machines are of the IBM variety.

Make sure you like the feel of the keyboard too. Some people prefer the noisy, clicky types. Others like the soft, mushy variety. You'd be surprised how a little thing like that can drive you mad.

Beyond that, there is the question of power. Potential computer buyers always want to know whether they should buy the latest 486 or make do with a bargain-basement 286. The size of the microprocessor is, in some sense, a measure of a machine's horsepower. The 486-based machines run Windows and other sexy applications. So do 386s, though perhaps not with blink-of-an-eye speed. The 286, as we mentioned, is probably not a good choice if you want to run the more advanced software. So which do you buy?

Wyckoff says, "My advice to anyone buying a computer today is to buy the best you can afford that will do the job." If you're only going to use the computer to draft an occasional memo or write a business letter, he says, a less powerful computer may do the trick—for now. The problem is, your needs are likely to change. You may someday require, or even prefer, more powerful multimedia applications, and you don't want to be stuck with a grossly underpowered computer. And with the price of a 486-type computer system, complete with color monitor and sometimes a printer, listing at substantially less than $2,000, it may prove to be a false economy to invest in a slower, dumber computer.

As for what brand to buy, Wyckoff prefers a particular mail-order manufacturer, Gateway, which he says uses high-quality generic components and comes preloaded with the buyer's choice of software, a very nice feature for the neophyte. However, other experts prefer better-known brand names. Mark Bunting, aka "The Computer Guy"—he has a syndicated TV show—tries to avoid off-brand computers, which he says may not use quality components. "My problem with some off-brand computers is that they may *seem* more competitive in price," he says, "but that's because they're using subquality components."

No matter whose computer you want to buy, look for a good warranty. One year is the industry standard, but you can do better. A few models have warranties extending as long as 18 months or even three years. Wyckoff also recommends that you seek out the largest hard drive you can find for the money. A bigger hard drive gives you more available disk space, the better to store all those supercool applications. By the way, many dealers will install your applications for you—for a price. Find out before you buy.

Should I buy a laptop?

If you need to use a computer only occasionally, and especially if you tend to be on the road a lot, a laptop may be for you. But if you plan to work at it all the time (even when you're not traveling), says Wyckoff, it's probably not a wise choice. For one thing, he says, they're more costly than desktop models. "You pay about a 50 percent premium for a laptop," he says. "Smaller is almost always more expensive." Another drawback of most laptops is that they can't be expanded. With many of the new desktops, if a more robust microprocessor comes along you can remove the old one and replace it. Not so with laptops.

Some laptops "dock" into a desktop chassis, but, again, these are more expensive.

Do I need gadgets like modems, fax/modems, or faxboards?

If you plan to gain access to the office mainframe and communicate on E-mail, a modem is a necessity. Buy the fastest one—measured in terms of baud rate—you can afford. A fax/modem or faxboard, which sends and receives faxes, can be useful if you understand its limitations. You can't transmit original documents, says Wyckoff, unless you have another accessory, known as a scanner, to "read" documents into your computer. This adds to the cost. Without a scanner, fax/modems only transmit documents contained in your computer's brain. "Very seldom are fax/modems cost-effective," Wyckoff says.

GTE's Joe Hearn recommends that users who are interested in fax capability wait just a bit longer. Fax prices are going to drop soon, he says, perhaps making a faxboard or fax/modem irrelevant.

Should I buy a laser printer?

Only if you really need very high quality printouts, says Wyckoff. Most of us can make do with a conventional dot-matrix printer, now available at reasonable prices and capable of higher-quality printing than machines on the market even a few years ago. Another option is an ink-jet printer, which offers higher-quality printouts, comparable to laser, at a price only slightly higher—around $400—than high-end dot matrix. If you're an architect and you have to provide sharp, colorful, highly detailed printouts, however, says Wyckoff, "you'd better be prepared to pay the freight."

Computer Mishaps

No matter which computer you buy, you still may be concerned about the potential for computer glitches and bugs. If these mishaps occur in the office, there is often a systems support person to help you out. You might also rely on that person should your computer crash at home—though obviously problems aren't as easily resolved long-distance. And no doubt about it—disasters do occasionally occur. I once lost a 6,000-word story on deadline—I still don't know how—but using a popular disk utility program, I was eventually able to find all of it, in bits and pieces, hiding on the hard drive.

But in Wyckoff's experience, most users have little to fear. "Computers are dumber than dirt, and they are schizoid. They'll do things you can't explain," he says. "But the amazing thing to me is not that computers occasionally break; it's that they don't break far more often. You've got gazillions of tiny little components inside microprocessor chips. There are a million transistors on a 486 chip just an inch and a quarter square. A computer operating at 33 megahertz is doing 33 million things every second. The laws of probability say they're going to break. And yet, compared to cars, which only have a few thousand parts, they rarely do."

But nevertheless, you should use a surge protector to safeguard the computer against power fluctuations and buy some antivirus software, particularly important if you're going to be transporting disks from your home to work and back again. Antivirus software acts like a kind of hunter-killer satellite, searching through your computer disks for computer viruses—bits of programming inserted into a system by a hacker with the sole intent of sabotage—and neutralizing them. Software like this would have come in handy for me on a Friday the 13th a couple of years ago, when a virus invaded my files at work and blew out most of them.

A Few of Their Favorite Things

In many of the conventional offices where I've worked, management had strict rules about how I could decorate my work space, right down to the maximum size and number of photographs I could place on my desk. Wall hangings of any sort, whether photos of the family trip to Disney World or Day-Glo Jimi Hendrix posters, were forbidden.

But in your home office, you can pretty much decorate in any way you please. Here are a few favorite home office items cited by telecommuters in my own informal survey:

Ray Tanner, group travel agent: "My comfy chair. It rocks, it's soft, and it spins in all directions. It has wheels, so I can roll it across the floor. I can spin around and reach things on my bookcase. I can turn in the other direction and reach my file cabinet. When I'm at home, I never have to leave my comfy chair."

Charlene Blythe, financial planner: "I have a bird feeder mounted on the outside of my window. It's a nice distraction. I also have a few toys, including a beautiful doll, on my bookshelf. To me, these homey little touches say 'There's someone with a personality who works here.'

Harry Humes, poet and English professor: "My favorite thing is an old lapboard. I cut it out of a piece of plywood a long time ago. I lay it across the arms of my easy chair when I want to write. If I count anything as lucky for me, it's that old lapboard."

Jerry McGrath, data entry clerk: "One of the things I dislike about the main office is the restriction on decorations. So at home I let it all hang out. I have a plastic blow-up model of a Klingon battle cruiser hanging over my desk and a large, stick-on, glow-in-the-dark photo of the moon. It looks great when I turn out the lights."

Bruce Boyer, men's fashion expert and consulting editor for Town and Country*; author of* Eminently Suitable *(W. W. Norton, 1993):* "I can think of three things I find indispensable in every conceivable way. I do love my answering machine. It frees me up. I can go take a walk and get away from the office, which I love to do, and then, when I come back, I have the world outside waiting for me at the press of a button. I'm of an age where inventions like that impress me. Having worked without one for so long, I can see how it's changed my life for the better. Another little office accoutrement is my daily desk diary. I don't write anything, usually, but business items in it. I write everything down. It gives me an incredible feeling of security. The other thing I like is the cordless phone, since I like to work in the yard."

Chapter 8

The Boss Said Yes. *NOW* What?

When you work in your office each day, though you probably take it for granted, your time and behavior are highly structured. You start at 8:30 A.M. You leave at 4:30 P.M. You might be expected to park in a particular section of the company lot. You have 45 minutes for lunch, which you must coordinate with your colleagues to make sure the phones are covered. You have two breaks. Your personal phone calls are limited. You are not allowed to smoke in the building. Jeans may be your favorite apparel, but the company mandates conventional business attire.

Structure can be confining, even stifling. But if you stop to think about it, structure can also sometimes be comforting and reassuring because there are few unpleasant surprises. You know what is expected of you from one moment to the next. Everyone, at least in theory, is treated in the same fair manner. If you have to be at your desk and plugging away by nine o'clock, then so does everyone else. If you have to wear a tie—even though the air conditioning in your building is on the fritz and the windows don't open—then so do all the other guys.

Now, if you're a highly motivated, well-organized individual, as most successful work-at-homers tend to be, maybe you don't need the structure of the office to help you do your job. Perhaps you get everything done by five anyway. But some people, when they begin working at home, find that something is missing. They drift. They don't know what to do first. Or they try to do everything at once. They take too many breaks, or they take none at all. They find themselves spending too much time looking in the refrigerator. (See *Lead Yourself Not Into Temptation* later in this chapter.) In the absence of structure, some feel cut adrift from their traditional moorings.

Of course, if you have negotiated a work-at-home arrangement with your firm, you probably do have at least *some* structure. For instance, you may be obligated to be at your desk and reachable by phone during certain hours of the day, no matter what personal schedule you have set for yourself. Your job itself may be a highly regimented one, such as taking catalog orders for JC Penney or responding to rider inquiries like the customer service reps for Phoenix Transit. But for those who have more creative, information-based jobs that deal essentially in the business of ideas, there is probably more freedom to decide the proper at-home organization of work and time. This is comparatively more difficult when your projects are long-term.

Regardless of the type of work you do, effective self-management is essential. Here's a step-by-step guide to making the transition from flying with the rest of the flock to flying solo.

Step One: Steady as She Goes

One of the main reasons people want to work at home is the need for some measure of personal freedom. They may want the flexibility to cram eight hours of toil into six highly concentrated hours, with time left over at the end of the day to take the kids to soccer practice. They may prefer being able to work at a more leisurely pace from ten to four, go for a workout, and then work for another two hours later that night. However, at least in the early going—and until you have convinced yourself and your company that you can be trusted to work unsupervised—you would do well to mimic the more restrictive organization of the formal office setting.

"In the beginning you have to have a lot more organization than you might have otherwise," says Jan Dean, a Fort Worth home-based business consultant and founder of a firm called the Well-Organized Woman. "You have to set up some pretty strict guidelines to get you through the transitional phase, from the well-ordered environment of the traditional workplace to the relatively unstructured environment of the home." (See *Avoiding Professional Pitfalls,* Chapter 6.)

Start With a Schedule

If you haven't given the notion much thought, Dean recommends that you begin by setting up a strict schedule that mirrors your regular schedule at the main office. Get up at the same time you normally would. Shave, shower, and have breakfast. Get the kids off to school. Plan to begin and end work at the same time every day. Take lunch and breaks at the same times you would if you were in the main office.

Add Flexibility as You Go

You certainly aren't obligated to continue in this conformist vein forever—or what would be the point? You can be a drone just as easily at the office. The whole aim of this exercise is to ensure that you get your work done—proving to your employer that you *can* be trusted to get your work done—while you take time to get comfortable with the new reality of being at home. This is a period to get to know yourself better. So stick with the standard schedule for a month or two. Then, says Dean, you can gradually begin to experiment with earlier or later starting times, or compress all of your work into a more compact block of time, or come up with some balance of housework and *work* work that best suits your needs.

"Once you get through the transitional period, you will find out the whole world isn't going to collapse if you don't stick to a rigid schedule," says Dean. "You will get to know and understand your own personal work style, and you can begin to play with the schedule, getting to the point where you feel you are being most effective."

Step Two: Discover Your Personal Work Style

I know this about myself: I tend to be at my most creative in the afternoons, and I work better in small chunks, with little breaks to have a cup of tea, make the bed, marinate the chicken breasts, or take a brisk walk down the avenue. I'm usually far less productive in the morning. I'm slow getting started. For that reason, I fill my mornings with what I call "getting ready" rituals. I make a pot of tea. I empty my trash can, which is usually overflowing from the day before. I read the *New York Times*. I erase last month's files from my disk. I draft memos. I call my writer friend Denise to exchange gossip and complain about the state of the world.

More on the importance of rituals later. But first, what we're talking about here is not *what* you do when you work, but *how* you do it. How and when do you work best? Under what particular circumstances are you most imaginative, creative, and productive? What is your personal work style?

For Jan Dean, the most productive part of the day is the morning. "In the afternoon my energy level is the pits," she says. "That's when I dust my office and clean out the files, all the things that need to get done but don't require as much thought."

Perhaps up until now you haven't thought about your work style. To Dean, that's not surprising. "When you work for a corporation, your work style is *their* work style," she explains. "But when you're on your own, even though you're still working for them, you're learning to do things according to your own schedule. As you work, you learn a lot about yourself."

Keep Track of Your Pace

But to make that knowledge valuable, Dean adds, you have to pay attention. Keep close track of your at-home hours for the first month or two. It might help to write down what you do and when you do it. You may find, for example, that you do your work-related housekeeping at certain times during the day. Or you may notice that you characteristically enjoy a burst of creative energy between three and five in the afternoon. Perhaps you find that after lunch you are sluggish and unproductive. Chart your activities and then choose a weekend to review your progress. Note when you produce the most and when you might be better off concentrating on some of the no-brainer, administrative work.

And keep an eye out for trouble spots, says Dean. "Be honest with yourself," she recommends. "If you find that morning goes by and you haven't accomplished anything, or if you've spent a large part of your day puttering around the house, you know you have a problem. Analyze those problems and make another list of how you're going to solve them."

You may find, for instance, that you use housework as a way of procrastinating. Clearly you either have to learn to avoid doing the chores until you are done with your work or think about returning to the main office. Dean recalls the story of a famous writer who always worked in bed. "She used to say that she made it a point never to get out of bed while she was working," Dean recalls, "because she could always find something to dust." Or perhaps you are easily distracted, flitting from one task to another. You need to concentrate on time management, about which you will soon learn more.

Make another list, while you're at it, of some of the other, more personal activities in your life that are important to you. Perhaps, like many telecommuters, you like the idea of being able to pick up the children after school and spend an hour or two with them before dinner. Maybe it's important to you to spend an hour three mornings each week running or bicycling. Compare this list of personal activities with your list of professional activities, and try to come up with a combined personal-professional schedule. You may decide to stick with nine to five. Or you might discover that if you get up at six and sit down at your desk immediately, you can get in eight hours of work in plenty of time to collect the children.

Once you understand how you work best, you can then begin to develop a new structure to support that mode.

HOME ALONE

You may seem like the ideal candidate for work-at-home. You're a driven, highly motivated, well-organized person, a dyed-in-the-wool self-starter. But the ability to work in an organized fashion, without direct supervision, is *not* the only requirement for home-based work.

Consider Janet Behre, who in June 1993 took a sales job with a major telecommunications company. In this job it was her responsibility to persuade business customers to sign up for long-distance service with her company. Janet, who says she always enjoyed getting out to meet customers, really liked the sales part of her job. Her problem was with another aspect of the business.

Most telecommuters have to have an established work record with their firm before they are permitted to work at home. But at her new company, Janet began working at home every day, practically from the start. The company was squeezed for space and wanted to require its salespeople to work from their homes. Janet was supplied with a laptop computer and a printer, and a separate telephone line just for company business. In the beginning it seemed ideal.

"I knew when I accepted the sales job that I was going to be expected to work at home," she recalls, "and I really liked the idea. I had been in sales before, in a position where I had to report to the office at certain times during the day, but the rest of the time I was on my own, going on sales calls and meeting with customers. So I looked forward to it, and I thought I understood what I was getting into." But as the weeks wore on, Janet quickly realized that her home-based lifestyle was at odds with some very important personal needs. Janet had good home-based work habits. It wasn't that she was disorganized. She was just plain lonesome.

"Everything about my personality suggested that I would be ideal for working at home," she says. "I'm self-motivated and very highly organized. But I found that being self-motivated wasn't enough to keep me going. It turned out that I was very lonely on my own. It really started to get me down. I talked with my boss about coming back into the main office, but this was more trouble than it was worth. The only space available were these office 'cubes' that didn't really belong to any particular person. I had the option of coming in and working in one of these cubes, but often it wasn't easy to find one of them empty. Besides, all my files were at home. It was impractical to lug them back and forth."

Janet found that the best part of her workday was when she went out on sales calls. She found that she relished the opportunity for person-to-person contact—the kind of relationship that was altogether lacking with her supervisor and colleagues. She felt isolated, and soon her unhappiness began to spill over into her personal life. Her friends began to pick up on her gloom. "I felt bad for my friends," she says. "But I really had a hard time separating my work from my personal life."

Adding to Janet's misery was the fact that she could never escape her job. She lived in a one-bedroom efficiency in Fairfax, Virginia, with her computer and all of her files and working papers piled up in the living room. The apartment was too small for a separate workspace. "The 'office' was always there," she says. "Sales can be a never-ending job. You can always think of one more contact to call. I felt like I was always obligated to do stuff, to follow up on leads, on the weekends."

Just possibly, an effective screening process might have determined that, in spite of surface qualifications, Janet Behre did not have the right stuff for working on her own. "Some people just shouldn't be telecommuting," explains Joanne Pratt, one of the nation's leading corporate telecommuting consultants. "Sometimes the space isn't suitable, or sometimes they don't have the equipment they need."

Loneliness is, for some telecommuters, a problem serious enough to justify ending the experiment, says Illinois telecommuting consultant Beverly Addante, founder of Telecommuting Works. "I draw a distinction between being alone and being isolated," she says. "When you're home alone, you can acknowledge to yourself that you are alone for a purpose, because you're doing a particular type of work that requires all your concentration. But when you feel isolated, you may think the whole world has forgotten you, and that's a different feeling altogether." If you have a sense of isolation, she says, that's a signal that perhaps you should be spending more time in the main office.

Linda Risse, a principal in the Virginia-based consulting firm of Synergy Planning (which advises companies on how to set up flexible workplace programs), says experiences like Janet's demonstrate that most telecommuters need to limit the number of days they spend at home. "A lot of people aren't prepared for the loneliness," she says. "We help companies train potential telecommuters, and they are sometimes surprised by what work-at-home entails. When it comes right down to it, I tell them, not everybody's cut out for it."

Clearly, Janet Behre was not suited to be on her own every day. Late in her employment with the company, she was shifted to a job inside the corporate office, working on special projects. But by that time, Janet had already been out looking for a new job. Two weeks after she started in special projects, she left the company. But in those two weeks Janet learned for certain that she wasn't cut out for the isolation of an everyday work-at-home arrangement. "Those two weeks in the main office were the happiest I had ever been with the company," she says.

Step Three: Manage Your Time

Being aware that you are most effective between nine in the morning and noon, or after seven at night, is just the beginning. Now that you know when you work best, you need to lay out a step-by-step procedure for getting your work done during these times.

Break Up the Day

Consultant Beverly Addante recommends that home-based workers manage their time in clearly defined blocks. It doesn't matter, she says, whether the blocks are from eight in the morning till noon and from one till six or if they're one-hour blocks related to specific tasks, just as long as you get into the habit of setting specific goals for the time allotted. Then, when you've completed your assigned task, reward yourself—in any way, Addante says, that does not involve food.

Think of rewards that refresh you or give you energy—not ones that weigh you down. Take a walk to the library. Read your E-mail. Play a workout video. "This is the beauty of working at home," says Addante. "You can arrange your time to take advantage of the home environment. You can use the home environment to support your creativity."

Keep Lists

On more of a micromanagement level, Addante recommends that you become an avid list-maker, if you aren't one already. Write everything out in detail, hour by hour: "At 10 A.M. I'm going to respond to my E-mail. At 11 I'm going to call my prospects." And so on.

One telecommuter I know keeps a large blank space open on her desk, which she fills with three-by-five cards at the beginning of each day. Every card bears information about a task to be completed. As she finishes each task, she throws the appropriate card into the trash can. This tells her at a glance what remains to be done, and it gives her a visual measure of progress as she goes through the day.

Jan Dean lives by her spiral notebook calendar, and she uses Post-it notes to keep lists of her tasks and when she has to complete them. I use a variation on that theme, writing out my tasks for the day on Post-its that I place across the top of my computer screen like tiny signal flags. I toss each one after I get the particular job done.

I also keep a separate list of tasks on a legal pad, simply because I'm compulsive, along with *another* list that bears the names of people I've phoned who have yet to call me back. Next to each name goes a brief notation explaining why I want to talk with them. If you speak to a lot of people during the day, as I do, you've probably had the experience of drawing a blank when someone returns your phone call. I even occasionally record personal reminders on my home voice mail, which can be programmed to call and remind me of scheduled interviews and appointments.

All of this may strike you as a little extreme, but I regard list-making as a kind of security blanket. Now you *might* be able to get along with one or two hastily jotted notes. But for most of us, some kind of system is required. Says Beverly Addante, "If you aren't organized, you can't make it at home."

Be Task-Oriented

Ted Merlo, who works in telephone directory product management for GTE in Irvine, Texas, says he realized from the very start that he needed to be organized to work at home. "The key for me was learning to plan my day," he says. "I found that you really have to do that in order for working at home to be effective. Once or twice I didn't plan ahead as well as I should have, and I didn't feel that I got as much done." And, he adds, it isn't enough simply to say to yourself "I'm going to use this day to return phone calls or write memos." You have to spell out clearly each task that you expect to tackle in a given day.

The day *before* your scheduled work-at-home day, figure out what you're going to need to take home with you in order to get the job done. And get together with your boss to talk about what you expect to get done on your day—or days—at home. Set goals and benchmarks. The fact that your boss knows what you plan to do reinforces the need to adhere to those expectations, and it offers the bonus of making your supervisor feel more secure.

Step Four: Commit Yourself to the Task at Hand

You'll probably like working at home, but you might not always like your work. Perhaps you've drawn the office drudge assignment, some mind-numbingly dull, achingly tedious, but nonetheless absolutely necessary bit of paper shuffling or twit work. You might be tempted to put off the task or drag your feet. But what happens when that job isn't done, or at least isn't done to the satisfaction of your supervisor? If you were working in the office, you might be able to justify your tardiness by saying you got dragged off to a long meeting. You could say that you were interrupted by the sudden emergency down in the production department. But when you work at home, you should have none of the usual office distractions, and it will be much harder for you to justify—or, let's be blunt, make feeble excuses for—your inability to complete the onerous and much-dreaded task.

Stay Motivated

If you expect to survive, and even thrive, at home, you have to maintain a high level of enthusiasm for your work, even when it isn't always your cup of tea, says Beverly Addante. "You have to be fully invested in what you are doing, in your job as a whole," she explains. "You have to be totally committed, and commitment takes in the whole issue of passion—that is, how much you like what you do." You have to work through some of the rough spots at home, she says, and keep your eyes set on the big picture.

Remain focused on the intrinsic rewards of your business or profession. Don't worry so much about succeeding as a telecommuter in order to satisfy the company. Concentrate on succeeding because it makes *you* feel good.

Lead Yourself Not Into Temptation

Picture *you,* the trusted home-based worker, reclining on the couch, lazily tossing back bonbons and watching *One Life To Live.* This is an image that fills every boss's heart with fear. The dread suspicion that you might not attend to your work may be one of the main reasons many supervisors resist the notion of home-based work. They worry that you might be distracted by all the comforts of home—the TV set, the refrigerator, the garden, the backyard pool, or the nearby community tennis courts.

No question about it: Some people do fall prey to distractions. Consultant Linda Risse, a member of the Virginia Governor's Telework Advisory Task Force, says she always warns potential telecommuters, "Some of you will have a problem every time you walk past the refrigerator or the cupboard."

(As perhaps the primary mid-Atlantic consumer of Cheez-it crackers and microwave popcorn, I can vouch for that.)

Again, not everyone is an ideal candidate for home-based work. If you're easily distractible, maybe you would be better off in the central office. But it doesn't have to be that way. Here are some expert tips on avoiding temptation:

- Make certain that your work space is physically separate from your living space. "Don't work in the kitchen, your bedroom, or in the living room," says Risse. "Your office should be a distinct space with a door you can close."
- Keep the television out of the office.
- Alert your friends, family, and neighbors to the fact that you

are at home and on the clock. Ask them to avoid calling or dropping in during particular hours.

- Keep to your personal schedule.
- Keep nonbusiness items, like the latest Jackie Collins bodice-ripper or the family exercise bike, at bay. They don't belong in your office. And even though your computer hard drive may have the capacity to store nifty games, store only business applications.
- Don't use your office for nonbusiness family or personal activities during your scheduled work time. Your office is no place for your children to do their homework after school. Don't allow your work space to serve double duty as a sewing room or a hobby shop for your spouse.
- Although it is tempting to relax your usual professional standards when you're out of the office, resist the urge to make personal phone calls.
- Schedule housework for before and after work or during your breaks. You might get to the point where you're easily able to toss a load of laundry in and then go back to work. But for some of us, the laundry is a reminder that the recycling needs to go out, the gutters need cleaning, and so on.
- Have everything you need for your work within arm's reach. The moment you have to leave your work space to do or get something, you expose yourself to the possibility of unwanted distraction.
- Anticipate child-care and even pet-care needs. We've said it before, and we'll say it again. You probably can't work with a toddler yanking at your pants cuff. Put small children in day care, or bring a sitter into your house. If the children are older, make sure they understand your rules. That is, when the office door is closed, Daddy or Mommy is working. (For more advice on coping with kids, see Chapter 9.)

Step Five: Institute New Rituals and Rewards

Most of us have little rituals to help us get ready for work and for going home. When we get to the office, we brew a pot of coffee. We go through the mail. We bop over to the cubicle next door to exchange a choice bit of office gossip with a colleague. We check our messages and, in various ways, clear the decks. At the end of the day, we duck into the boss's office for a quick update. We pack away all our pens. We file away all the paperwork.

Whether or not we realize it, rituals are important. They set psychological boundaries around our work, psych us up for the day's labors, and help us wind down in preparation for the long trip home.

But what happens when home *is* work? What then? Some experts believe that the case for rituals is, if anything, even stronger for those of us who take work home. In the absence of the commute to work or the usual office chitchat, we need to substitute new ways of getting started and wrapping up.

Rituals for Getting Started

"Some people start their day by going out for a jog," says Beverly Addante. "Others drop their children off at day care or read the paper. To them, that signals that the workday is beginning."

Consultant Linda Risse, in her presentations to prospective telecommuters, recommends strongly that, at least in the beginning, workers try to adhere to at least some of their old customs. "Get up at the same time you always do when you go into the main office to work," she advises. And as tempting as it might be to avoid shaving or to work in your ratty old robe, Risse recommends against it. "Get dressed—maybe not in the same clothes you would wear if you were going into the office to work, but in neat attire.... This helps you get your mind attuned to the fact that you are going to work."

Take Time for Little Social Rituals

And keep the rituals going throughout the day. If it's normally your practice to head down to the cafeteria at 10:15 for a cup of coffee with your friends, you might plan an informal coffee klatch with your next-door neighbor—although you should be on guard against this practice becoming too much of a distraction.

For some workers, an important starting and ending ritual might be spending a few minutes schmoozing with an office pal. If you're working at home, a little gabbing might help keep the feeling of isolation away. So if it helps and it is a part of your normal ritual, Risse says, give your colleague a phone call. But again, be careful. "Taking a few minutes out of your day to chat with a co-worker may be a normal part of your ritual," she says. "This can be perfectly fine. It's a tool. It makes getting started easier. If it increases your productivity, do it. But don't forget to ask your co-worker if he or she minds. And if you think it's wasting time, this is your opportunity to stop unproductive behavior and change the way you do things."

To guard against overwork, Risse and others advise that you also develop closing rituals. Turn off your computer. Turn out the office lights. Close the door.

Step Six: Keep an Eye Out for Trouble

Every few weeks or so, stop and evaluate your progress. Are you meeting goals? Are you being creative? Do you feel content? Or do you feel like you've been abandoned?

Be self-monitoring, suggests Beverly Addante. "You have to make an effort to increase your self-awareness about your productivity, about your energy level. Watch for trouble signals. Do you have the feeling you aren't getting anything done? Maybe you just don't feel as alive."

These could all be signs that perhaps you aren't the telecommuting type—or that you need to spend more time communicating with others, perhaps in the office. Maybe you need more feedback from your supervisor. But whatever you do, don't give up. There's probably a good, healthy balance of work and home for everyone.

STRUCTURING YOUR AT-HOME TIME

- At first, keep to a schedule that's similar to your regular office routine until you are used to managing your time.
- Figure out when your energy and concentration levels are highest, and plan to do the bulk of your work at that time of day.
- Organize your workday by keeping lists, planning, and working in well-defined blocks of time.
- Keep motivated. To get through the rough and the dull spots, remind yourself of the reasons you enjoy your job. Take pride in your work.
- Use daily rituals to help you gear up for and wind down from each workday.
- Periodically evaluate your productivity, your energy level, and your enthusiasm to determine whether your work-at-home arrangement is really right for you.

Chapter 9

When Home and Work Collide

"Working at home is, for some people, so unusual that they have a difficult time understanding it," explains Kathy Faber, a writer and editor for a central Pennsylvania publishing company. "It just doesn't stick in their heads. They think you're either working *or* at home—but you can't be both."

And so it rarely surprises Kathy when acquaintances drop by with what probably seems to them like a perfectly realistic request. "One of my neighbors in the part of town where we used to live once called and asked whether I'd mind watching her son for an hour while she went shopping. I had to tell her no. Most people understand when I remind them that I'm on company time," she says. "But you have to remind them a lot. Even my husband doesn't always get it. He asks, 'Can you pick up the dry cleaning? Can you drop off that check?' Sometimes if I'm not real busy, I can. But often the answer is just no."

As Kathy's experience suggests, people who work at home often come face-to-face with other people's perfectly *un*realistic expectations. To some of your friends and family, you may be regarded as something alien. You are neither fish nor fowl. They may wonder why you can't go to the office or the plant just like everybody else. Why can't you just have a normal job? Family members—children in particular, but sometimes full-grown spouses too—may not take you at your word when you say you want no interruptions. "Does that *really* mean you don't have time to talk about the basement waterproofing now?" Some family members just might not comprehend that when you are home, locked away in your office, you really are *at work*. To them, if you're home, you're just "off." (And they mean that in the nicest possible way.)

No matter how long you work at home, there will always be someone—family, friend, neighbor, or delivery person—to attempt to draw you away from your labors, disrupt your concentration, or derail your train of thought. While home can be a refreshing escape from the more rigid, formal atmosphere of the main office, you may encounter—or even inadvertently generate—quite unexpected friction with your loved ones.

But the pressures and demands of work do not necessarily have to conflict with the quite unworkmanlike distractions and amusements of home and hearth. Like many home-based workers across the country, you can negotiate a peaceful, fair, and balanced settlement with friends, neighbors, and relatives.

Working, With Children

There are two scenarios to consider here: trying to work while tending to very small, constantly needy children, and working while keeping an occasional eye out for older, somewhat self-sufficient kids who may need no more than an occasional hug. The first situation can prove very nearly impossible; the other may be doable, depending on the children in question.

Small Fry

We've already noted that it is tough to function as a paid professional when you have small children to care for. A number of companies with formal telecommuting programs—Pacific Bell, for example—expressly prohibit the use of home-based work as a substitute for more suitable child-care arrangements. Of course, most people who work at home don't labor under such restrictions. And some of them *are* able to blend work and child care, though with some difficulty.

Kathy Faber, who works most days at home, reporting in to the office only occasionally, is one telecommuting mom who successfully maintains her career standing while caring for her child. Andrew, six, is in kindergarten, but he is enrolled in a morning program, which means he arrives home at about 12:30. Andrew is home for several hours in the afternoon when Kathy is hard at work. Fortunately for Kathy, Andrew is mature enough to play without the kind of intense direct supervision and involvement required by toddlers, who are—as befits their age, temperament, and level of maturity—more clingy and dependent.

"Andrew is almost always very good about not bothering me while I am working," Kathy explains. "Like a lot of six-year-old boys, he is usually more interested in whatever he is doing than in what *I'm* doing. I have to keep an eye on him, of course, but he sometimes goes next door to play with his friend, or his friend comes here. That probably seems like it would be more work, but it really isn't, because they play well together. As a result, Andrew is less likely to get bored and come looking for me to be his playmate."

Occasionally Andrew slips and interrupts his mother when she is on the telephone. Fortunately, Kathy frequently writes about pediatric issues, so she finds herself talking with pediatricians and child-development specialists—who are more understanding than others might be. "I make it a point to tell some of my contacts ahead of time that I have a small child at home and that we might be interrupted," she says. She concedes, however, that she "might be able to get away with that because I'm a mother. A man might not be able to."

Kathy also makes time for her child-rearing responsibilities by working a determinedly rigid schedule, starting early—usually around 7 A.M.—and working straight through until 3 P.M. "I'm a really well organized individual," she says. "I can usually do in 20 hours the things that other people do in 40 hours. When I'm at home, I don't mess around. If I were in the office, it probably *would* take me

40 hours. The work tends to expand to fit the time and space allotted. But at home I don't have that luxury."

Kathy's experience notwithstanding, most home-based workers are inclined to make other child-care arrangements (see *Who's Watching the Kids?* later in this chapter). No matter how mature and well-mannered your children may be, you probably know that their maturity and their manners have limits. You may need to place your child in day care for at least part of the day or bring someone into the home to help with child-rearing responsibilities. And it probably ought to go without saying that spouses, if they are home, should do their fair share of minding the kids. But more often than not, some arrangements must be made. Telecommuting consultant Linda Risse puts it bluntly: "You cannot work and take care of small children. That's a given."

Connecticut draftsman Matt Diefenderfer, who hired a sitter to care for his three- and five-year-old children while he worked at home, agrees. And he took extra measures to make certain the kids would respect his privacy. "When I first began working at home, I put a lock on my office door," he says. "It might seem heartless, but after a few months the kids got the idea."

Bigger Fish

Older kids are another matter. Generally, if they are old enough to walk home from school and cross the street alone, they're probably mature enough to take care of themselves at home—with some reasonable amount of supervision. However, they must also be old enough to understand the rules of your at-home workplace. It may not be realistic to leave them to their own devices, and even an older child is certainly capable of interrupting old Dad at inconvenient moments. One editor I know who wasn't able to curb her kids' Pavlovian phone-answering responses began unplugging the phone in her kitchen when she was working so the kids couldn't answer it.

In the view of Beverly Addante, founder of Telecommuting Works, your after-school arrangement with your children should be structured, but with plenty of leeway for dealing with the occasional homework crisis or stopped-up toilet.

"You should take care to make distinctions between unwanted outside interruptions and interruptions from your children and other family members," Addante says. "You have to try to be available occasionally and to be clear about when those times are. You have to get in the habit of making promises, like 'Between three and four I'm not so busy, and I'm available to you.' Kids need an occasional hug, and they need to know when's a good time for that and when isn't. And if you get in the habit of making promises to your children, you have to keep them."

You may also find that your children are not happy about your occasional inability to respond immediately to their needs. However, says Addante, parents should explain to their children that, insofar as their needs are concerned, the fact that Mom or Dad works at home is a trade-off. On the one hand, you aren't always with them, even when you're in the same house. On the other hand, a lot of older children come home to an empty house or spend time in after-school care. This way, at least Mom or Dad is around. "My children know I'm there for them," says medical underwriter Marylee Newman, "as opposed to my not being there at all, and they don't want to jeopardize this arrangement any more than I do."

Adds consultant Linda Risse, "Tell your kids, 'There may be some things about this arrangement you don't like. Maybe the TV will have to be on softer. But on balance, we'll have some extra time, and I'll be there in case of emergencies. This is a big plus for our family.'"

One other thing to look out for: Don't treat your kids like employees. Occasionally home-based workers emerge from the office and don't quickly make the transition out of work mode into home mode, points out University of Wisconsin researcher Sherry Ahrentzen. They begin barking orders to the children and expect the kind of instant compliance and lockstep efficiency they're used to at work. But children aren't employees, and they aren't slaves to a time clock. They're not on any particular schedule at all. So take some time to decompress before leaving the home office—remember the importance of end-of-the-day rituals (see Chapter 8)—and cut them some slack.

Finally, don't expect your children to be perfect little angels. Ellen Galinsky, co-president of the Families and Work Institute, a nationally recognized nonprofit research and planning organization in New York, says that if you try to make your expectations clear to your children, assuming they're mature enough, they'll usually behave. However, she warns, "you'll always have some hassles around the edges."

Who's Watching the Kids?

Any parent of small children who has worked at home will tell you: Work and kids just don't mix. Three-year-olds don't understand deadlines. They don't appreciate grown-up responsibilities. They only understand that, in the absence of verifiable scientific evidence to the contrary, they are the center of the universe, and everything—the moon, the stars, the planets, and Mom and Dad—revolves around them.

Some work-at-home parents *do* manage to maintain a balance between work and child care. But as this survey of 104 home workers by Sherry Ahrentzen, associate professor of architecture at the University of Wisconsin, suggests, most people make other arrangements. Here's who takes care of the kids when a parent is working at home:

A baby-sitter or day care	25.7 percent
A spouse or companion	22.9 percent
Themselves	17 percent
Themselves and a spouse or companion	20 percent
Themselves and a baby-sitter	5.7 percent
A spouse or companion and baby-sitter	5.7 percent
Other	2.9 percent

Source: *Blurring Boundaries: Socio-Spatial Consequences of Working at Home,* Sherry Ahrentzen, University of Wisconsin-Milwaukee, School of Architecture and Urban Planning, 1990.

CHILD-CARE SOLUTIONS

If you're determined to succeed in your home-based experiment, you'd better not try to include child care in the mix. Here are some options:

- **Early to work, early to quit.** If you have school-aged children, or even toddlers in day care, plan to begin your workday at about 7 A.M. Then work straight through until school's out.
- **Hire some helping hands.** One home-based writer I know hired a young college student to mind her one-year-old boy, Max, during core business hours—10 A.M. to 3 P.M. The busy writer also required that the sitter be willing to answer the phone, do some filing, and handle correspondence.
- **Put your kids' maturity to the test.** Assuming you have children old enough to understand what it means when Daddy or Mommy puts out the Do Not Disturb sign, you may be able to function at home with only occasional interruptions for real emergencies, like rescuing the cat from the trash compactor. Give the kids a two-week trial. See how well they conform to your desire for solitude. If they seem to manage on their own without causing you too many disruptions, and without setting fire to the carpet, they pass the test; they can be trusted. If not, you'll have to consider some other child- care arrangements.
- **Reward them.** On the one hand, Mommy or Daddy is home. For kids who are mature enough to be home when you are, that's always a better proposition than spending the afternoon in after-school care or, for older children, in an empty house. On the other hand, even though you're home, you aren't always available for them. Don't forget how much they need you. When they've been especially good, take them to a mati-

nee. Treat them to a Happy Meal. Plan a picnic supper at the playground. Make them equal partners in your success.

Husbands and Wives

Dan Olasin, president of two geographic information companies, divides his time between offices in northern New Jersey, central Pennsylvania, and his home in rural Wellsboro, Pennsylvania. He spends about two days a week working out of his house, which he shares with his wife, Regina, a public health physician. They originally lived in New Jersey, closer to one of Dan's companies, Intelligent Charting, Inc., but moved to Wellsboro in 1986 so Regina could accept an assignment from the Public Health Service to direct a number of local health centers. They have no children.

Because of his wife's responsibilities, Dan says, Regina works odd hours. Dan himself is an avowed workaholic who until recently labored seven days a week. "There are times when I'm available and she's not, and vice versa. Sometimes she's on call for a night and we aren't able to spend the evening together, or she's available but I absolutely have to get some work done."

Dan and his wife have to make a special effort to structure time together, and he can see how home-based work could be an unhealthy, all-consuming effort. "It would be very easy, if you had problems in the marriage or the family, to use your office as a place where you could avoid facing those problems," he says.

Linda Risse agrees. "If you're going through a divorce or any kind of stressful situation in the family," she says, "working at home may not be the best thing for you now."

Home-based work can provide more time for tired, harried marrieds. But as Dan Olasin suggests, home-based work can also bring out the worst in workaholics. Already-neglected spouses may not look with fondness on their partner's desire to open up a corporate branch office in the spare bedroom. Work-at-home arrangements may also pose problems in terms of changing expectations—"Now that you're home, you can keep up with the laundry"—or unanticipated turf wars.

Make Sure You've Got Your Spouse's Support

All the more reason, says consultant Beverly Addante, for prospective home-based workers to have a long heart-to-heart with their spouses before pursuing the new arrangement. "It isn't always a simple call," she says. "You have to make sure those around you really support you. Sometimes they don't. Often you get to know things about people you love that you never knew before." For example, some potential telecommuters are surprised to learn that their spouses resent their decision to turn the only spare bedroom into an office, leaving no place for Pop-Pop to sleep when he visits from Grand Rapids. These bones of contention should be gnawed over long before you bring your work home with you.

"When you start to work in the home, you are invading the existing territory of the household," says Dallas consultant Joanne Pratt. "It might be a good idea, ahead of time, to ask who you might be displacing. [Your family] may not view your coming home to work with the same delight as you. You may have to make the case that this arrangement has benefits for them."

Pratt continues, "I once interviewed a man who was working for US West, now GTE, a middle-level manager whose job was writing curriculum materials for company training. He took a lateral transfer, and as part of his new job he worked at home every day. It turned out his wife really didn't like it at first. But after a while she realized that his being home meant that she didn't have to be there every day at three when the kids came home from school."

Another important note: Make it clear that your work-at-home arrangement doesn't necessarily mean you'll have time to take up more of the household responsibilities. In a recent, as-yet-unpublished survey of 17,000 telecommuters by Joanne Pratt, she finds that "one of the most striking differences between the men and the women is that the women typically expected men to help with the housework" when the men began working at home. It's *possible*—but neither you nor your spouse should count on it.

Neighbors and Relatives

As researcher Sherry Ahrentzen's findings suggest (see *Could Ya Keep an Eye Out for the Repairman, Hon?*), neighbors and relatives do not always understand or appreciate your need to remain focused on your work.

While no friend or neighbor would presume to drop in to your office in the city, some will misread your new home-based status as a signal that you aren't as committed to your job on the days when you are home. Relatives are no less guilty of this presumption, though with them, as with all your family members, you have to react with a greater degree of patience and understanding, says Linda Risse.

Could Ya Keep an Eye Out for the Repairman, Hon?

Some people just don't get it. Even though you're home, you're working. And yet the doorbell rings, and it's your pesky neighbor with yet another friendly little request. Fortunately, most neighbors rarely or never interrupt home-based workers while they're on the job, according to researcher Sherry Ahrentzen's survey of home-based workers. Of those who *do* ask neighborly favors, here are some of the most frequent requests:

- Accept delivery of important mail or parcels
- Take care of the neighbor's kids
- Keep an eye on the home while the neighbor is away
- Perform unpaid business favors
- Run errands or give the neighbor a ride somewhere
- Let service or repair people into the neighbor's house

Source: *Blurring Boundaries: Socio-Spatial Consequences of Working at Home,* Sherry Ahrentzen, University of Milwaukee, School of Architecture and Urban Planning, 1990.

Telecommuter and Crestar benefits compensation executive Donelle Glatz believes she has come to grips with this often ticklish problem. "My mom will sometimes say to me, 'Thursday is your day off.' Or my friends will say, 'Let's go to the mall or the park.' As tempting as it is to do something else, I have to politely say no and remind them that I've agreed never to be away from my phone or unavailable for more than two hours at a time."

Whatever you do, don't assume you're being nice by telling intruders that you aren't really busy or that what you are doing at the moment isn't important. It *is* important, and others have to know this or they will keep on asking. Sherry Ahrentzen comments, "Sometimes a neighbor will drop by to say 'I'm not going to be here today. Will you keep an eye out for a UPS delivery?' It may not seem like an imposition to them, but they would never think of asking you such a thing if you were in a big office, with a manager looking on. If you don't stop them right away, those favors can become cumulative—a favor one day, then another a few days later, and so on."

"You have to tell people that your telecommuting arrangement is a privilege," says consultant Linda Risse. "Let them know that you are getting paid for your time at home. This will usually work in every case except for overbearing people." And those people, she says, have to be told in no uncertain terms: "I'm working."

Home Survival Tips

- Before you sign on for a work-at-home program, meet with your family and determine how they feel about your being at home two or three days during the week.
- Just because you are home doesn't mean you will be able to do all of the housework. Make certain your spouse understands this with crystal clarity. If anything, your spouse may

be required to pick up more responsibilities—for example, taking over bedtime chores while you work.

- At the same time, don't be distracted by housework. When you're home all day, two or three days a week, you're more likely to notice that the refrigerator needs cleaning out or that there are dust bunnies living under the bed. It's all too easy to be drawn into tackling some of the housework, and if you are very disciplined you just *might* be able to do a little more than usual. However, housework is, or can be, never-ending. It might be better to pretend you didn't notice the dust and let the bunnies have the run of the place until you aren't on the clock.

  Travelers programmer Janet Reincke says, "As part of my orientation program we were told that you kind of have to ignore your surroundings—the dirty dishes and so on. I make it a point not to let housework get in the way. It's really too much to do both, to concentrate on your work and do all the housework too."

- If both spouses work at home, this can be a very cozy arrangement—a little *too* cozy. Make certain you have worked things out so that you aren't both going to need access to the computer at the same time or your spouse isn't doing a lot of noisy, chatty phone work while you are trying to concentrate.

  Pacific Bell systems design consultant Cheri Shore and her husband, Bob Grenader, who is self-employed, share an office in their home. They have two L-shaped computer tables butted together to make a big T, with the computer in the middle. "Usually we don't conflict," says Cheri. "A good deal of the time I'm out visiting my client, the Jet Propulsion Laboratory, and when we're both in the home office and need the computer at the same time, we have a laptop that one of us can use."

- If you have small children in the house, arrange for someone else to watch them, at least during the part of your day when you are most absorbed in your work. Although it might be possible to care for an infant while on company time, consultant Linda Risse says, "once they get the idea that Mom is home and they want to play, it's time to do something else with them."

- If your children are older and more mature, they may be capable of being at home with you while you're working. However, they may be unhappy that you're not always available to shoot baskets or walk to the corner store with them. Assure them that a caring Mom or Dad is around, if not with them every minute.
- Put up a sign on your office door that reads, simply, Office. Or perhaps Mom At Work. Reinforce the notion, for your children and for your significant other, that this room is like no other room in the house, and that while the door is closed, interruptions are discouraged.
- Adjust your schedule so that you get most of your work done early in the day, say, between six and two or seven and three. Then, you still have a few hours of daylight in which to attend to your children or pop dinner in the oven.

  Ellen Galinsky of the Families and Work Institute, a leading expert on workplace flexibility, worked just such a schedule when her son was still very young. "I got up at four every morning, wrote for two hours, and then spent time with him," she says. "Then later on when he took his nap, I would write for two or more hours. Fortunately he was a big napper."
- All work and no family is usually an unworkable compromise. The fact is that you *are* home, and your children *will* occasionally want to speak with you or even ask you for a hug after a rough day at school. Get into the habit of spelling out which times are best for family interaction and which times are most troublesome. Post the "available" times on the door. If you promise your son or daughter that you will be accessible from 2:45 to 3:30, or whatever, do keep your promise. And, as telecommuting consultant Beverly Addante says,

don't make promises you aren't sure you can keep.

- If a spouse, a neighbor, or a very close relative of mom rank or thereabouts is always calling, dropping in, or asking you to run errands, you must nip those presumptions in the bud, tactfully but firmly. Say, in so many words, "I can't talk now. I'm being paid for this time, and if I talk with you now, I'll have to make up the time later or I'll miss an important work deadline."
- A home answering machine might help you to screen your calls. Another option is a phone service like Ident-a-ring, which I described in Chapter 7.

Chapter 10

Take It on Home Now

There are reasons for working together as a group and reasons for being apart. If we can become more sophisticated in our work, we can design it so we may be apart for the kind of work that can best be done that way and be together for the kind of work that requires that we touch base.

Suzanne Smith, co-director of New Ways to Work

The nature of work is such that we are blurring the boundaries. What we are seeing is, in my opinion, a move from the industrial age to the information age, from a situation where we once worked together to a new realization that, with new technology, we can work anywhere.

Joanne Pratt, Joanne H. Pratt Associates

My first computer was a Commodore 64, a grossly underpowered toy compared with virtually all of the machines now on the market, but when it was first offered, it was state of the art. In just a few short years, computer technology has come an incredibly long way. I can do things with my relatively low-tech 286 IBM compatible that I never dreamed of doing with my old clunky 64. I can remember, too, transmitting my Three Mile Island stories by facsimile from the Pennsylvania Statehouse to my newspaper in Levittown. The fax machine was an awkward revolving drum that scanned printed pages slowly and unreliably. Today I have a far more reliable faxboard plugged into my computer. It cost me less than a hundred bucks.

The technology now largely exists for more and more workers to leave the comforting womb of company headquarters and to head out into the exurban frontier. The obstacle to home-based work, then, isn't a lack of technology; it's old, muddled thinking. We have the way, but American enterprise lacks the will. We know that telecommuting works. It's cheap, effective, and often highly creative. Still, companies resist. This isn't how we do things, they say. We've *never* done things this way.

You have an opportunity to change that stubborn mindset. Perhaps you even have an obligation. As so many telecommuting experts and administrators have pointed out to me, home-based work solves many problems, not the least of which is the need for worker flexibility. Just breathe in the fumes during rush hour on a hot summer day in Phoenix, or Gary, Indiana, or Atlanta. The need for sensible alternatives to the car is literally written on the wind.

So before you say "I can't" or "they won't," consider the time and energy wasted in your long commute downtown. Think of all the pointless inefficiencies of the office. And take another look out the window. Can you afford *not* to work at home?

Your Seven-Point Work-at-Home Action Plan

1. **Size up your suitability.**

The first order of business is to determine whether you're a suitable candidate for working at home. Take another look at the jobs and tasks listed in Chapter 2 that are well suited to home-based work. If it seems that some or all of your job can be performed at home just as easily as in an office building, working at home might just be a possibility for you.

But it isn't enough just to think you might be a good candidate. First you have to consider why you want to work at home. Make a list of what's in it for you.

Making a list of reasons is useful because it helps you come to grips with reality. If you're really honest with yourself, you might discover that you're not a good candidate. Better to find out now rather than later, when your job, and the future of all telecommuting at your firm, may hinge on the outcome of your noble experiment. But for many of us, making a list prompts us to think hard about what we do for a living and to discover that, for many aspects of our jobs, the office is the worst place to be. We may determine that working at home means working better—and working smarter.

2. **Lay the groundwork.**

Make another list, this one including all the reasons your proposed work-at-home arrangement might benefit your employer. Think mostly in terms of tangible business benefits and much less in terms of soft, "touchy-feely" human resources justifications.

One way to advance your argument might be to link your proposal to federal clean-air requirements. Or suppose your company is growing by leaps and bounds, creating the need for more office space. Point out that by sending more workers home, your employer might be able to save on space.

Remember, in the eyes of the average boss, the most obvious impact of your proposal on the business will be, simply, that you won't be there. If you really want to get what you want, you have to demonstrate in the clearest possible terms how your absence helps, rather than hinders, business.

3. **Gather supporting documentation.**

Throughout the country, more and more companies are exploring telecommuting. Some of the largest and most influential companies have already done a lot of your homework for you, and they have plenty of experience. Go to your public or corporate library and search through the business magazines and newspaper data bases (if your library provides such services) for articles on companies that have telecommuting policies. (For an example of such a policy, see Chapter 3.) Seek out information on telecommuting at companies like Bell Atlantic, Pacific Bell, the Travelers, JC Penney, the federal government, and others mentioned in this book. Write to the human resources department for information.

Finding out what other companies do and how they do it will give you a good idea of how to frame your proposal. Pay particular attention to companies within your industry. If you can find any good examples of competitors who offer the work-at-home option to their employees, even if only on an ad hoc basis, you may be able to point out that this places them at a competitive advantage vis-à-vis employee recruiting.

Your employer may also feel more secure knowing that your company will not be the first to take the telecommuting plunge.

Read *Home Office Computing,* the definitive popular journal of home-based work. And cruise through some of the human resources journals for articles that support your case. This is a hot topic.

Several influential organizations, like Link Resources and the Conference Board, have taken an active interest in the emerging phenomenon of home-based work, along with other workplace flexibility issues. Write to them for information. Such groups regularly churn out useful reports with detailed facts and figures. (Some of these reports are listed in the appendix.)

4. **Anticipate objections.**

Now you've finally got all your ducks in a row. Will they float? A lot depends on how well you've done your homework. But in the final analysis, bosses may not be impressed by your keen understanding of this new workplace trend or altogether wowed by your arguments.

In spite of what you might believe—or what they might have you believe—bosses are thoroughly human. They have worries and fears, some of them firmly grounded in reality. Like "What will happen to my job if I try this new idea and my employees are found sunning themselves at the beach?"

Chief among bosses' less rational fears is the notion of employee invisibility. Or, "How can I possibly manage an employee whose face I cannot see?" The answer to that fear, although it may take some selling, is management by objective. What's important is not whether your boss can see you, but whether you produce.

Meet your boss's cold, unreasoning fear head on. Say "I know you're worried about whether I'm going to be working when I'm at home. But if I can give you assurances that I *will* be working, would you at least consider the idea?"

If the boss says yes, be prepared to commit to a written agreement that spells out the details of your work-at-home arrangement. It may include some or all of the following provisions:

- You agree to be at your desk and reachable by telephone at certain core periods during the day or agree to carry a pager so you can be contacted any time, anywhere.
- You will achieve certain benchmarks. If you are a claims representative for an insurance company, for example, agree to resolve a given number of claims in a week or a month. If you don't meet these goals, it ought to be easy for your boss to verify it.
- You will meet with your boss regularly. On the afternoon before your day at home, get together with the Big Cheese and go over your plans. Then meet again on the day you return to the office and bring him or her up-to-date.
- You will not use your day at home for child care. (Though depending on your circumstances, your boss may be flexible about this.)
- You will be flexible. Agree to be in the office for special events, meetings, crises, and so on. If Thursday is normally your day at home and the supervisor calls a sales meeting on that day, you will not throw a hissy fit. You will be there.
- You are prepared to make concessions. Some companies will let employees work at home but won't supply computer equipment. If you want to work at home badly enough, you'll consider any reasonable concession. By the way, agreeing to a cut in pay is *not* reasonable.
- You will leave an escape hatch. Let your boss know that this agreement can be terminated at any time, by either party.

The important thing—and this is crucial—is that you do your job with no noticeable disruption of the office routine. Grind out the work. Prove you can be trusted. If you do that, most supervisors will begin to lay their fears to rest.

5. **Be on your guard.**

Some people are so grateful for the opportunity to work at home that they go overboard trying to prove their worth. But while it's true that a sweatshop mentality may appeal to your supervisor, you can't possibly hope to maintain that pace. In no time at all, you'll be wiped out. And then you'll begin to look back to your old days in the main office with longing in your heart.

There are ways to work smarter. Do the following:

- Maintain a regular schedule—restricting yourself to a sensible number of hours.
- Take five. You need to seek respite periodically. And develop end-of-the-day rituals that help you get out of work mode.
- Avoid isolation. Make an effort to stay in touch by phone when you're out of the office. And don't be a stranger. Just because you're scheduled to work at home doesn't mean you have to miss all the unofficial company functions that enhance work relationships.
- Stay on the agenda. As I mentioned before, make sure you remain flexible enough to attend official company meetings and business functions as required.

6. **Plan your home office.**

You're going to spend a lot of time in your home office. You'd better be comfortable with it. If you're stuffed into a remote corner of the basement where you feel like just another spud in the root cellar, then you are not going to be very happy. And you will likely be unproductive. Nor would such a work space be held in high regard by the company. Some firms won't even *let* you work in such a location.

Before you begin your work-at-home adventure, take time to think about your space and equipment needs.

Start by planning ahead. Think now about where you want to work. What is the best space you have available? What is in it now? Who or what will your office displace, and will any other family members (notably, your spouse) be unhappy about being edged out?

What kind of equipment, if any, must go into your home office space? Is there enough room for it? Is the office far enough away from the usual household traffic?

Before you move into your new space, give thought to your communications needs. At the very least, you should have a phone answering machine or the telephone company's equivalent of home voice mail.

Finally, carefully consider your computer needs. Maybe you'll conclude, as many home-based workers do, that you don't need a computer. Maybe your firm is going to supply whatever equipment you need. If you do need a computer, think about compatibility. Does your firm rely mainly on DOS-based computers or on Apples? Generally, don't buy an IBM if your office uses Apples, and vice versa.

Consider, too, how you plan to use your machine. Do you only use your computer at work for writing the occasional memo, or do you use it for producing the company newsletter? Your use may dictate your choice of computer.

7. **Adopt effective work-at-home habits**

When you work at home, you get to write your own scenario. When do you start? How long do you work? When do you take a break? How should you dress? Do you have to work eight hours at a stretch?

Yes, you *can* do what you want—the desire for a small measure of freedom is one reason most people want to work at home. But there are rational limits to your liberty. You can't sleep in until noon, work for a couple of hours, and go play miniature golf for the rest of the day. You have to do your work, or this gig's going to end pretty quickly. But you do have the freedom to choose variations on the usual workaday theme.

If you've never worked independently, you may not know the best way to work at home. Until you do, it might be a good idea to work roughly the same schedule you normally would. Try keeping a log during those first few weeks. Maintain a record of what you do when. You may discover, if you didn't already know, that you work best at a certain time of day.

Another crucial element of your work-at-home program is the ability to develop, and religiously adhere to, schedules. How you do this is up to you. Use three-by-five cards, a calendar book, or some nifty computer program—but by all means, map out the course of each day. If you can't keep to your schedules and meet your personal deadlines, telecommuting isn't going to work for you.

Finally, it's easy to get so bogged down in your work that you lose sight of why you wanted to work at home in the first place. Stop every once in a while and think about how lucky you are. You're home in comfy clothes while everyone else is marooned on Dr. Moreau's Island of Suits and Ties. You can take your dog for a long walk in the park when you want to. You can avoid the horror of commuting. If the mood strikes, you can take your paperwork out onto the deck and sip lemonade while you review sales figures. So stay focused on what working at home does for you, and you'll do what you have to do to keep the boss happy.

Nothing Ventured, Nothing Gained

Before wrapping things up, I want to talk to you about possibilities. If you have never worked at home, and you don't know anyone who has, telecommuting can seem altogether *im*possible. It is remarkably easy to look at your company or your supervisors and halfheartedly conclude that "they'll never go for it." Of course, if that's what you think, then maybe they never will.

Before I negotiated my first work-at-home agreement, I remember thinking along the same negative lines. I can recall worrying that the boss would refuse. But that was not my worst fear. I also worried about how our relationship might change if he did refuse and I had to keep to my in-the-office schedule. After all, my supervisor might well reason that an unhappy employee who wanted to telecommute but couldn't probably wouldn't function at the same high level as when he was happy. Or he might think that a truly miserable and desperate employee would probably start looking for another job. And, just maybe, my boss would tell me to start looking.

All sorts of nightmare scenarios played out in my mind before I decided to propose working at home. Although things turned out all right in the end—my supervisor didn't scream or yell or tell me I was a lunatic—I believe I took a calculated risk. I made the pitch to my boss after I had been on the job only 14 months. But if you've been around much longer, your relationship with your employer probably runs somewhat deeper. There may be more understanding and trust. You may find it easier to spill your guts when you're unhappy.

If your ties with the boss are not as tight, you can reduce your exposure to risk by being well prepared and open to compromise and, most of all, by not being confrontational. You shouldn't present your case in either/or terms. Don't state or imply that if you don't get what you want, you'll take a hike.

If it makes you feel more secure, work through an intermediary. For example, find a member of your human resources staff who is up-to-date on workplace trends and propose that telecommuting be studied as a possible alternative to the same old nine to five. Offer yourself as a volunteer to both research and test the idea. Finally, if you truly are insecure—or your company isn't known for its openness to new ideas—you might find safety in numbers. Discuss your idea with co-workers who share some of your concerns about long commutes, inadequate family time, and flexibility, and work on a proposal together.

But by all means, throw off those negative thoughts. They drag you down and keep you from realizing your dreams. All around the country—indeed, throughout the world—workers are redefining the terms of their jobs. Understand that there is no difference between you and them.

Well, one difference, perhaps. They did it. They banished the word “impossible” from their vocabularies. What’s stopping you?

Appendixes

APPENDIX A

READINGS

TELECOMMUTING CASE HISTORY
PACIFIC BELL
MAY 1985–JUNE 1989

Pacific Bell's telecommuting program is designed to provide employees with an alternate work style while maintaining established objectives as agreed upon at the outset by the telecommuter and the respective supervisor. The program provides a method to assess the implications of telecommuting and assists clients in configuring and implementing programs tailored to their individual needs.

Participation is available to all managers throughout the corporation at the discretion of their supervisor. Current participants include marketing account team members, engineers, marketing planners, programmers, analysts, project managers, external affairs managers, technical support managers, and forecasters. The pilot program began in 1985 with 75 work-at-home telecommuters and 22 telecommuters working from two satellite offices. The program has increased to 590 work-at-home participants and 25 satellite office participants. An additional 400 participants have been identified as using the concept informally.

Two satellite offices are maintained and house multidiscipline employees. The locations of the satellites are San Francisco and Woodland Hills. Each office can accommodate 15 employees. The work-at-home participants are located throughout the state of California.

There have been no special arrangements implemented regarding support personnel in the office to assist the telecommuters. Remote workers have access to the same centralized administrative support group as their office co-workers. Participants are encouraged to establish a buddy system so that the telecommuter has someone in-house to call with job-related questions.

Financial compensation for telecommuters remains the same as for their in-office colleagues. Benefits coverage for the telecommuter is also status quo.

Distribution of employees practicing telecommuting is:

Financial management	45%
Operations	33%
Sales	15%
External affairs	4%
Networking engineering and planning	1%

Evaluation

Pacific Bell considers telecommuting to be a viable management work option that, when appropriately applied, benefits both the company and the individual. The ongoing responses are positive and promising. Pacific Bell continues to monitor the progress of the telecommuting program. Results of the two most recent evaluations are as follows:

- The three primary reasons for telecommuting are:

1. To cut commute time or hassle	55%
2. To work at my own pace	27%
3. To save transportation expense	27%

- The telecommuters noticed significant increases in the following four areas:

Area	Percent indicating an increase has occurred
The quantity of my work	63%
My feelings of satisfaction with my work	71%
My feelings of satisfaction with my home life	57%
The amount of time I spend working	70%

- Some of the advantages of telecommuting include:

Increasing the amount of work produced	87%
Having fewer distractions	75%
Feeling less job-related stress	57%
Having the ability to work their own way	52%

- The disadvantages mentioned most often are:

Working too much	26%
The lack of support tools—clerical and equipment	32%
Reduced interaction with co-workers	28%

- More than eight out of ten (85%) of the telecommuters consider themselves successful telecommuters.
- Almost all of the telecommuters (96%) were satisfied with telecommuting.
- Seven out of ten employees (69%) thought their boss had a favorable evaluation of telecommuting. Very few respondents (6%) felt their superiors viewed telecommuting with disfavor.

The summarized results of the supervisor survey are as follows:

- The majority of managers (38%) are supervising three to five telecommuting subordinates, and most of the managers (70%) have supervised telecommuters for a year or more.
- There are a variety of methods the supervisors are using to communicate with the telecommuters. The most popular methods are:

Electronic mail	90%
Communication via telephone	87%

Face-to-face meetings	83%
Voice mail (voice message, retrieval, and storage system)	57%

- About one out of four supervisors (28%) feel that managing telecommuters is more difficult than managing in-office employees. The concerns most frequently mentioned were:
  - Assessing work performance
  - Communication problems
  - Maintaining a sense of teamwork
- A number of ongoing expenses associated with telecommuting were identified. The three most common expenses are:
  - Telephone lines
  - Office furniture
  - Terminals/PCs
- Two out of three managers (67%) noted that increased employee satisfaction resulted in higher productivity. Other benefits include:

Reduced absenteeism	57%
Increased productivity	42%
Reduced stress	42%

- The majority of supervisors (61%) state that managing telecommuters is no different than managing in-office employees, and some managers (6%) feel that telecommuters are easier to manage. Managers who find that supervising telecommuters is easier also stated that this was due to the satisfaction their employees feel from telecommuting.

Summary of Results, July 1989

In July 1989, the Telecommuting Task Force launched a study of Pacific Bell managers (telecommuting and non-telecommuting) to identify the nature and extent of current telecommuting practices in the company; to quantify the strength of managers' interest in telecommuting; to determine what factors influence decisions to telecommute or not; and to identify attitudes and beliefs toward telecommuting. Questionnaires were mailed to a random sample of

6,256 managers stratified by department; 55% were returned within the three-week period of field work, and an additional 4% were received too late for tabulation. Principal findings include:

- **Incidence of telecommuting.** The number of telecommuters at Pacific Bell may be as low as 5% or as high as 17%, depending on whether one looks at how people perceive themselves or what they actually do. Without being given a definition, 9% of the respondents claim to be "telecommuters"—either in their boss's judgment (4%) or their own (5%); this group telecommutes an average of five times and 30 hours per month. Using supervisors' estimates of telecommuters reporting to them, 5% of managers below division level telecommute periodically. However, looking at actual behavior, in May, at least a third (35%) of the managers who didn't name themselves "telecommuters" spent at least some time working at home as a substitute for normal office hours. Most managers worked at least 15 hours at home before they called themselves telecommuters. However, some managers who say they are not telecommuters work at home as much as self-designated telecommuters. Whether they called themselves telecommuters or not, in May, 17% of managers reported working at home 15 hours or more.
- **Incidence of work-at-home.** Two-thirds (68%) of managers report having worked at home during the last six months as a substitute for or in addition to regular office hours. Non-telecommuters working at home have made a significant personal investment already in computers (40%) and modems (15%). About half (54%) of non-telecommuters working at home have personally paid for work-related calls.
- **Commute patterns.** Telecommuting is perceived as a viable solution to traffic and pollution problems, a belief reinforced by the fact that 77% of managers drive to work alone, many with long commutes. Six in ten have one-way commute times of more that 30 minutes. Half of present telecommuters and nearly half of managers "very likely" to telecommute (45%)

must drive more than 45 minutes. Encouraging telecommuting in the company is seen as consistent with the company's external market posture and as a means to enhance the company's ability to attract top-notch talent.

- **Interest in telecommuting.** A substantial number of managers (59%) express "very strong interest" in telecommuting.
- **Potential telecommuting understood as part time.** "Likely" telecommuters do not think of telecommuting as a full-time assignment: The average anticipated telecommute time was about seven days per month. Interest in part-time telecommuting, preferably from home, is high—principally as a means of minimizing commute hassles, facilitating uninterrupted work, and addressing the stress imposed by the conflicting pressures of work and personal life. Results show that managers appear unable to make appropriate choices, based on the demands of their work, about whether and how often to telecommute.
- **Likelihood of telecommuting if offered the option.** Over four in ten managers (45%) say they would be very likely to telecommute on a periodic, part-time basis during the next 12 to 24 months, if offered the option to do so. Another 26% would be "fairly likely" to telecommute.
- **Reasons for telecommuting or not.** Managers generally decided not to telecommute based on reasons related to the nature of the work, particularly the need to be accessible to customers, colleagues, clients, subordinates, to office support, or to the communications network at the office. While it is clear that the desire to cut commute hassle is a strong inducement to telecommute, an equal number of managers (85%) said the desire to work without interruption was an important reason for this decision. Acquiring flexibility and control, reducing stress, saving transportation expense, and achieving a better balance of work and personal life are also strong motivators.
- **Beliefs about the effects of telecommuting.** According to managers, telecommuting will have significant and positive

outcomes for the management, employee, and company: Employee stress would be reduced (87%); job satisfaction would be greater (70%); and absenteeism would be less (79%). Employees would put in the same (40%) or greater (40%) hours, while productivity would be greater (64%) or unchanged (30%). It is believed that expenses would likely decline (48%) or stay the same (26%). Most felt company liability risks would be unaffected or decline (76%). Some managers expressed downside concerns about telecommuting: 43% thought chances for advancement would be reduced; 41% thought information security risks would increase; and half (54%) thought resolving performance problems would be more difficult. While some mention was made of reduced accessibility by telecommuters (45%) and potentially greater intrusion of family matters in the workday (42%), in light of the positive rating of productivity, hours, and absenteeism, these do not appear to be major concerns. To place these results in context, it is worth noting that supervisors with actual experience managing telecommuters are significantly more positive than other supervisors about telecommuting's beneficial effect on productivity and hours worked.

Comments From Telecommuters

"With voice mail it is possible to do a great deal of work from virtually any location. I find that having a certain amount of freedom of location, dress, time, etc., permits me to think about my work problems more creatively. I often feel that the "office ethic" stifles innovation, and we need more ideas/innovations/new approaches from people, not less. Freedom from commuting and dress code are the two big pluses for me. Also, time to write and read uninterrupted. Having a pager helps me to be available at all times and locations. I wish I could telecommute—even retreat to remote locations—more. I would like to see more team telecommuting at informal sites to work on projects."

"The freedom to telecommute has significantly increased my job satisfaction and loyalty, reduced my stress level by eliminating a long commute (on certain days), and giving me two extra hours with my growing family. On days when I telecommute after a meeting in San Ramon, the company gains productive time because I get home much faster than I can get to the city [San Francisco]. The accessibility problem I've noticed with telecommuting is largely one of perception. I wear a pager, check voice mail, and have a telephone line, so I'm 100 percent accessible. However, it takes people a while to feel comfortable calling me at home. They believe they're 'bothering' me. This is changing over time."

"Telecommuting is a good thing to have available, but I think most people need to 'touch base' with their office co-workers at least one day a week. Otherwise you become too isolated, not part of the team."

"Having telecommuted for two years as part of my job and now occasionally...I believe it is particularly valuable. As silly as it may sound, I think one of the most valuable parts of telecommuting is the ability to get going without all the finessing, primp, and folderol. In my 28 years I have never seen a suit, white shirt, tie, or fancy dress do any work....When I telecommute, I'm up by 5:30, same as usual, but am working by 6:00 at the latest, usually 5:35. Normally I'll work till about 4:00, grabbing a sandwich from the refrigerator and not taking a formal lunch break. The company has gotten ten hours work, and I'm home two hours ahead of time. We both make out very well. I believe the majority of managers, allowed to telecommute, would use the commuting time to do company business, not their own. At some point, higher management has to give middle to lower management some credit for commitment, brains, and ability. It's called trust."

Prepared by Carol Nolan, Telecommuting Manager. Reprinted with permission of Pacific Bell.

Remote Control: How to Make Telecommuting Pay Off for Your Company

By Kathleen Christensen

Companies can institute telecommuting in four basic ways: programmatic division, company-wide policy guidelines, ad hoc arrangements with local supervisors, and independent contractor arrangements. Each has its benefits and drawbacks.

The Programmatic Division Model. This style of telecommuting carves out a programmatic area of the company—such as telephone sales or data entry—and targets it for telecommuting.

Under this arrangement, telecommuting can actually save capital costs: permanently switching a percentage of the work force offsite reduces the need for new facilities.

On the down side, the program can lose its value as a morale enhancer if the company fails to make the eligibility criteria explicit. Other divisions may wonder why the telecommuters were singled out for special treatment. Management must make it clear to the entire company that the nature of the division's work makes telecommuting necessary....

The Corporate Policy Model. A few companies have taken the concept of telecommuting even further, establishing policies that allow employees throughout the company to negotiate telecommuting arrangements with their supervisors.

Creating a corporate-wide telecommuting policy opens up eligibility across divisions, reducing divisional rivalries and enhancing the authority of local supervisors. On the other hand, even a fabulous corporate policy can be short-circuited by local supervisors who are threatened by the concept. An appeal process is necessary to ensure even implementation....

The Ad Hoc Model. In ad hoc telecommuting arrangements, local supervisors—without formal support from the company—privately approve employee requests to work at home. These arrangements generally cover a limited number of days a week, typically run for a finite period of time, and often correspond to a project deadline or a family need. Most employees working at home today are likely to be doing so under such an informal plan.

Ad hoc arrangements have a number of advantages. They allow flexible responses to problems or crises with a minimum of paperwork. High performers can earn special treatment from their local supervisors. And because the arrangements are unofficial, employees who feel left out can't complain about any specific company policy.

Of course, with no formal rules, supervisors can easily abuse their power. Employees and supervisors who are involved in ad hoc arrangements can become prime targets for whispering campaigns by disgruntled colleagues.

The Independent Contractor Model. In the first three models, companies use telecommuting to attract and retain valuable workers, reduce absenteeism, and perhaps cut overhead costs. All three models are designed to meet the needs of both the employer and employee; all are win-win models.

The fourth model, which entails turning employees into self-employed independent contractors when they move from office to home, can create a win-lose situation in which management wins at the expense of workers.

For some companies, the major impetus for telecommuting is to cut labor costs: a company can save 30 to 40 percent on each employee-turned-contractor because contractors are not entitled to regular benefits. Furthermore, independent contractors are hired only as needed, which increases staffing flexibility for the employer.

The price for short-term cost savings is a long-term erosion of loyalty and morale. In addition, switching employees to independent contractor status may leave companies vulnerable to legal challenges from the IRS and state courts.

Of course, picking the right model isn't enough. Telecommuting is not a viable alternative for all companies, even those that have the necessary technology already in place. To decide whether telecommuting is right for them, companies must weigh their goals against the personalities, skills, and needs of their employees.

12 Tips for Making Telecommuting Work

1. Create definite policy guidelines. Specify who is eligible for telecommuting, how long each agreement will be in effect, and expectations for contact with the main office.

2. Clarify bottom-line considerations. Establish goals that the company hopes to achieve with telecommuting—for example, to recruit and retain valuable employees, cut capital costs, or respond more effectively to market demands.

3. Provide training so that managers feel at ease with an invisible work force. Supervisors must learn to judge performance by productivity, not visibility. Management must set up evaluation procedures for the telecommuter.

4. Set a policy for telecommuting hours. Should managers require telecommuters to keep the same hours at home as at the office or should hours be based on the amount of work? The answer will depend on the job to be done.

5. Choose individual participants carefully. Motivating remote workers can be difficult, so it's important that telecommuters be self-starters who do not require continual in-person interaction with colleagues or management.

6. Do not promote telecommuting as the sole solution to child-care conflicts. Anyone considering telecommuting as a work-family option must realistically assess the demands of working at home amid competing family needs. For employees with children, telecommuting should be part of a larger company-supported child-care program.

7. Maintain the status of telecommuters as regular employees. Have them come in regularly to meet with supervisors and colleagues and to attend company-wide meetings. Include them in the firm's social activities.

8. Give telecommuters regular briefings on company plans and objectives. This helps reinforce the importance of work obligations to employees trying to balance various parts of their lives while working offsite.

9. Consider part-time arrangements. Many benefits can be real-

ized if employees work at home three days a week instead of five. Part-time telecommuting ensures employee contact with supervisors and strengthens access to the company culture.

10. Consider using telecommuting as a time-shift technique. If full-day telecommuting isn't feasible, companies can give employees the flexibility to shift an hour or two of work from the office to home. This arrangement can be especially beneficial for employees with children.

11. Implement telecommuting as part of a broader strategy of increasing work flexibility. Telecommuting can be one option among many. Explore other alternative work arrangements that are suitable for the company.

12. Proceed with caution. Begin with a pilot program serving a limited number of participants for a specific period. Create management focus groups or task forces to discuss issues that arise. And make sure that employees' expectations of the program remain realistic.

Reprinted from *PC Computing*, February 1990. Copyright © 1990, Ziff Communications Company.

APPENDIX B

A LIST OF BOOKS, PERIODICALS, AND OTHER SOURCES

BOOKS

The Best Jobs in America for Parents Who Want Careers—and Time for Children, Too, by Susan B. Dynerman and Lynn O. Hayes, Rawson Associates, New York, 1991.

Described as "the first complete guide to locating, negotiating, and managing" flexible careers, *Best Jobs* was written by two high-level managers who shared a position as director of communications for a hotel corporation. The book examines all the possibilities for professionals who want a better balance between work and home, from telecommuting to job sharing to flextime—and more. The authors also include a helpful list of the 25 most flexible companies in the U.S.

Creating a Flexible Work Place: How to Select and Manage Alternative Work Options, by Barney Olmstead and Suzanne Smith, AMACOM, New York, 1988.

A largely human resources–oriented guide to a wide variety of flexible work options—flextime, compressed workweeks, part-time employment, job sharing, phased retirement, and, to some degree, telecommuting. A trifle academic in places, but you couldn't ask for a more thorough exploration of the topic.

The Home Office Book: How to Set Up and Use an Efficient Personal Workspace in the Computer Age, by Mark Alvarez, Goodwind Press, 1990.

A very detailed, illustrated book explaining the more technical aspects of setting up a home office, including useful information about hardware and software, peripherals, and other electronics, along with tips on office-space design and lighting.

Home Work: How to Hire, Manage and Monitor Employees Who Work at Home, by Phillip E. Mahfood, Probus Publishing, 1992.

The author makes liberal use of case histories, the better to enlighten and reassure skittish managers in the ways and means of telecommuting programs. He explains the advantages of telecommuting from the supervisor's point of view and suggests ways to manage remote workers.

The One-Minute Commuter: How to Keep Your Job and Stay at Home Telecommuting, by Lisa Fleming, Fleming Ltd., 1990.

Written and self-published by a well-known California telecommuting consultant, *The One-Minute Commuter* was one of the first books describing telecommuting. Offers advice on how to establish yourself as a telecommuter.

Organizing Your Home Office for Success, by Lisa Kanorek, New American Library/Plume, 1993.

Don't know how to keep your files straight? Overhead light giving you headaches? Missing deadlines, forgetting appointments? Kanorek's book gives you the skinny on how to turn your home office into a productivity tool.

The Telecommuter's Handbook: How to Work for a Salary—Without Ever Leaving the House, by Brad Schepp, Pharos Books, 1990.

Author Schepp, an editor for a research corporation, wrote this book when only three million Americans telecommuted. Still provides useful insights, along with a well-documented list of 100 companies in America that employ telecommuters.

Telecommuting: How to Make it Work for You and Your Company, by Gil E. Gordon and Marcia Kelly, Prentice Hall, New Jersey, 1986.

Written by work-at-home consultants, this book is geared toward supervisors, to help them learn to develop and manage work-at-home programs, stressing the difference between close supervision and *good* supervision.

Women and Home-Based Work: The Unspoken Contract, by Kathleen Christensen, Ph.D., Henry Holt & Co., 1988.

Based in part on Christensen's nationwide survey of more than 14,000 women home workers. Includes many illuminating, in-depth interviews with women—about their jobs, their lives, and how to balance the two. Presents an unvarnished view of "the realities behind the seductive images of home-based work."

Working From Home: Everything You Need to Know About Living and Working Under the Same Roof, by Paul and Sarah Edwards, Jeremy P. Tarcher, Inc., 1987 (revised).

One of the leading guides to the home-based work movement, with more or less equal emphasis on self-employment options and salaried jobs. If you find yourself interested in self-employment, a section on how to spot work-at-home schemes ("Sell fish bait and become a MILLIONAIRE!!!") is worth the price of the book.

Your Home Office: The Work at Home Guide to Success, by Norman Schreiber, Perennial Library, 1990.

A how-to book for entrepreneurs and salaried telecommuters,

filled with a good deal of technical information about setting up your office and purchasing the right equipment.

Reports and Surveys

National Work-at-Home Survey, Link Resources, New York.

If you want to know who's who and what's what in telecommuting, this is the definitive survey. Conducted by Link Resources, a New York–based research and consulting firm, this annual report describes in painstaking detail the full extent of telecommuting in the U.S. It offers specific information about the U.S. home-based work force and describes trends in electronic office product usage. If you're looking for hard numbers to back up your proposal for a home-based program, this report is absolutely essential. For information, write to Link Resources, 79 Fifth Ave., New York, NY 10003.

Work-Family Roundtable, The Conference Board, Volume 1, Number 1, December 1991.

This intriguing survey shows how companies are gradually becoming more flexible in their response to employees' family needs. It suggests that employees, not employers, are driving the new corporate flexibility. Available from the Conference Board, 845 Third Ave., New York, NY 10022.

Blurring Boundaries: Socio-Spatial Consequences of Working at Home, by Sherry Ahrentzen, University of Wisconsin-Milwaukee, School of Architecture and Urban Planning, 1990.

An excellent report exploring a cross-section of professional homemakers in a wide variety of jobs, from self-employed entrepreneurs to those employed by firms. It describes changes in the home as a result of the intrusion of work. Available from the University of Wisconsin-Milwaukee, School of Architecture and

Urban Planning, Center for Architecture and Planning Research, P.O. Box 413, Milwaukee, WI 53201-0413. Ask for Report R87-4.

Flexible Staffing and Scheduling in U.S. Corporations, by Kathleen Christensen, Ph.D., Research Bulletin No. 240, The Conference Board, 1989.

A highly detailed description of telecommuting and other programs in major U.S. firms. Though it is now somewhat dated, the report strongly supports "the need for new tools to manage flexible employees." Available from the Conference Board.

Newsletters and Magazines

Home Office Computing, Scholastic, Inc., 730 Broadway, New York, New York 10003.

Though the editorial focus is chiefly on the self-employed who work at home, a growing number of articles are devoted to those who draw a regular paycheck. Much of the information contained in this magazine, particularly product reviews, is quite useful to anyone who works at home, regardless of the circumstances. There's really nothing else on the newsstands that comes close.

The Telecommuting Review, Gordon and Associates, 10 Donner Ct., Monmouth Junction, New Jersey 08852.

A leading newsletter regularly and passionately devoted to the cause of telecommuting, published by consultant Gil Gordon. This is not a consumer publication but rather a high-level management resource with an appropriately high subscription price.

Articles

"Working at Home Pays Off," by Shari Caudron, *Personnel Journal,* November 1992.

"Telecommuting: A Better Way to Work?" by Bob Filipczak, *Training,* May 1992.

"Remote Control: How to Make Telecommuting Pay Off for Your Company," by Kathleen Christensen, Ph.D., *PC Computing,* February 1990.

"Worksteading: The New Lifestyle Frontier," by Roxane Farmanfarmaian, *Psychology Today,* November 1989.

"A Hard Day's Work in the Electronic Cottage," by Kathleen Christensen, *Across the Board: The Conference Board Magazine,* April 1987.

INDEX

D

E

About the Author

Jeff Meade has been a writer and an editor for many national magazines, including *Prevention, Children, Teacher,* and the American Society of Engineering Education's magazine, *Prism.*

He has spent much of his 20 years of professional writing and editing telecommuting from his Philadelphia home.